POCKET **ROUGH GUIDE**
MALTA & GOZO

written and researched by
JESS GERROW

CONTENTS

MALTA

Has any other tiny archipelago contributed so much to the history books? What sets Malta apart from other island destinations is the sheer number of historic sites, cultural attractions and ancient monuments squeezed onto its 246 square kilometres. With a dizzying number of World Heritage Sights for its size – inescapable reminders of its complicated 7,000-year-old-history – Malta feels like a huge open-air museum. But that doesn't mean it's stuck in the past; in recent years Malta has truly come into its own as an alluring, quirky and rewarding destination. An abundance of top-notch restaurants, charming villages, brightly painted balconies, bustling promenades, vintage cars and warm hospitality means this little island leaves a big impression.

The intricately decorated interior of St John's Co-Cathedral

The majority of Malta's historical sights are concentrated in Valletta and the "Three Cities," laid out around the Grand Harbour and marked by immense limestone walls. These impressive fortifications are a legacy of its complicated history, which has alternated between long spells of isolation and brief outbursts of momentousness during periods of conflict when Malta's strategic location at the centre of the Mediterranean gave it a significance disproportionate to its size. There are plenty of opportunities to get to grips with Malta's military past, with a host of impenetrable forts and several museums dedicated to the islands' crucial role during World War II and the Great Siege of 1565, when the Order of the Knights of St John repelled a six month attack by invading Turks. The Grand Harbour's fortifications enclose a host of extravagant churches and palaces, the legacy of the Knights, who ruled the island for the next three hundred years. While the Baroque designs of the Knights are ever-present, the Neolithic era made an equally significant mark on the islands. The magnificent

Statue of St Peter in front of the Rotunda

outdoor and underground temples across Malta and Gozo are the oldest freestanding man-made structures in the world, pre-dating Egypt's pyramids. Second to none, there are more major Neolithic complexes here than in the whole of the rest of Europe.

When to visit

The most popular time to visit is in high season (May–Oct). In July and August, when the Maltese also take their summer holidays, the island can feel suffocatingly hot and crowded, but it's a lively time to visit, coinciding with plenty of festivals and annual village feasts. Rain is nearly unheard of between May and September, and the countryside is parched and dry. Scorching temperatures make sightseeing difficult during midday, but evenings bring relief and life to village squares and promenades well into the night. Things get quieter in the low season (Oct–May), when the weather is mild, rain comes in intense but infrequent bursts, and the countryside is vividly green (though mosquitoes can be bothersome). The sea is too cold for swimming, but comfortable temperatures make sightseeing very pleasant. Outside of the high season, the best times to visit are the autumn or spring shoulder seasons. Festivals continue into the autumn and the sea remains balmy, while in the spring, the countryside is ablaze with wild flowers.

Terronne

A short boat-ride from Malta, Gozo has a more rural character than its sister island. What it lacks in the number of historic attractions of the mainland, it makes up for with tranquility, natural beauty and an amenable Mediterranean lifestyle. Hilly topography, ravishing coastal cliffs and striking salt pans offer marvellous walks, while the dive sites offshore are widely acknowledged as some of the best in the Mediterranean.

Though a small island it can take a while to travel on Malta's congested roads, even by bus (there are 6 cars for every 10 people on the archipelago). Malta's public transport system is modern and robust, servicing the entire country, including the sparsely populated countryside. Buses typically run from 5am to 11pm and cost €1.50 (winter) or €2 (summer) for a 2-hour pass. More economical and convenient is the Explore Card (€39), which offers 7 days of unlimited public bus travel and 2 ferry trips between Valletta, Sliema and the Three Cities. Travelling by foot or ferry can often be a faster option, particularly around Sliema, St Julian's and Valletta (be sure to make eye contact with drivers before crossing the road). Double-decker private hop-on hop-off bus tours are also a convenient for touring Malta's major attractions (€20, 1-day pass). Renting a car will free independent travellers to stray off the beaten path, but is not for the faint of heart. Driving styles here are aggressive at best and chaotic at worst, with road rules inconsistently observed and road conditions quite poor in some areas. However, reasonable rental fees (from €20/day) make this an economic option for families and groups. Renting a motorbike or scooter offers a faster way to bypass traffic on congested roads, but again, can be perilous. Cycling is just beginning to gain popularity in Malta and with very few bicycle lanes and a hilly topography, casual cyclists will find it nearly impossible to travel on two wheels (especially under the scorching summer sun).

Where to...

Shop

Undoubtedly, Malta's riches lie in its plethora of cultural attractions – not its shops – but there are a few gems to uncover amongst its monotonous selection of high street outlets and souvenir shacks. For your pick of handmade treasures head to Gozo, where artisan lace, reed baskets, leather goods and local delicacies are readily found throughout Victoria and the Ta Dbieġi Crafts Village. On Malta, you'll find a Mdina Glass shop in every major village; a sure bet for gorgeous glass creations. For fashionistas, Sliema and Valletta are the places to see and be seen, with shopping malls and a few boutiques from local designers.
OUR FAVOURITES: Souvenirs That Don't Suck, see page 60. Ta Dbieġi Crafts Village, see page 119. Charles & Ron, see page 41.

Eat

Dining out is an essential part of Maltese social life; according to national statistics, Maltese families spend just as much at restaurants as they do on rent and utilities. Unsurprisingly then, Malta is home to an astonishing number of restaurants: about 2300 at last count! Sliema, St Julian's and Valletta are brimming with mid-priced and upscale restaurants, mostly Mediterranean, Italian and Asian. Farther afield, local pizza, pasta and burger joints are reliable for cheap eats. A particular Maltese favourite is the huge, long and boozy Sunday lunch, served at almost every restaurant but particularly popular at sea or countryside outlets.
OUR FAVOURITES: Harbour Club, see page 43. Terrone, see page 103. Piccolo Padre, see page 62.

Drink

The ratio of bars to churches in Malta is easily three to one – impressive, when you consider the island is home to over 359 churches! Visit Valletta for atmospheric wine bars and elegant cocktail lounges (both often have live music), or Sliema for drinks with a view at its plentiful seaside kiosks. For a cheap pint in any village, the *kazin* (a marching band club-cum-community centre) is a favourite of locals. The Italian aperitivo tradition is alive and well in Malta; most drinking establishments see a rush of patrons from 6pm for aperitifs and small bites.
OUR FAVOURITES: Charles Grech, see page 45. il-Gabbana, see page 61. Hole in the Wall, see page 63.

Go out

The village of Paċeville, enclosed by sprawling seaside resorts and a small beach, is the centre of Malta's nightlife scene. Techno and hip hop clubs, British-style pubs and cocktail bars occupy most of its ten-block radius, making it a particularly popular destination for stag and hen dos. In the summer, the party scene shifts from Paceville to the massive outdoor club complexes around Ta Qali National Park, and the seaside lidos in Buġibba and Sliema, which compete to host the most impressive parties every weekend.
OUR FAVOURITES: Havana Club, see page 62. Hugo's Terrace, see page 63. Café del Mar Lido, see page 86.

Malta and Gozo at a glance

Gozo p.104.
With quiet villages clustered around gigantic parish churches, and a population whose hospitality is legendary, Gozo offers a peaceful, pastoral alternative to Malta. Unplug and unwind here while discovering rustic Gozitan food and a slower pace of life.

The north p.80.
With numerous small sandy beaches and a sparsely populated hilly countryside, the North is ideal for sun-seeking sojourns and peaceful hikes.

Mdina and Rabat p.64.
Mdina was first settled by the Phoenicians, but is characterised by its marvellous Arab-period medieval architecture, Baroque palaces and limestone cathedral. Twisting alleys have kept vehicles and modernity at bay here. Admiring the expansive views of the entire island from atop the citadel's looming fortifications, it's easy to see the strategic importance of this ancient capital.

Central Malta p.74.
So densely populated it's impossible to tell where one village ends and another begins, Central Malta offers few tourist attractions but an authentic slice of everyday life.

The south p.94.
Dramatic cliffs, colourfully quaint fishing villages and four Neolithic temples (the most stunning is the Hypogeum) make the south a must on any itinerary.

| 0 | miles | 2 |
| 0 | kilometres | 2 |

›mino p.122.
›e tiny islet of Comino is home to the
›nously crystal clear turquoise waters
the Blue Lagoon, as well as some
›enic coastal walks. The best time to
it is in the spring, when the rocky
›rigue habitat comes into bloom.

The Three Cities p.46.
Characterised by a medieval urban
fabric of close-knit Baroque
architecture, the "Three Cities" are
home to Knightly palaces and forts
handsomely contrasted by a more
recently constructed superyacht
marina.

Valletta p.26.
The churches, palaces, fortifications and grand public
buildings of Malta's capital city – designated a World
Heritage Site in its entirety – have remained largely
unchanged since their construction more than 450
years ago. Charming architecture, modern museums,
and Malta's best restaurants make Valletta an eclectic
and essential place to explore.

Sliema and St Julian's p.54.
Once a sheltered fishing village, Sliema was
the location of Malta's first holiday resort in
the 1970s, with St Julian's not far behind.
Today, this lively 5km stretch of coastline is
home to an impressive array of cafés, bars
and restaurants.

15

Things not to miss

It's not possible to see everything
that Malta has to offer in one trip
– and we don't suggest you try.
What follows is a selective taste of
Malta's highlights, from its Baroque
architecture to its stunning coastal
landscape.

> GOZO'S CITADEL
See page 106
Offering panoramic views of much of Gozo, and home to no less than four museums, a cathedral, and a superb interpretation centre, the compact, honey-coloured Citadel punches far above its weight.

< VALLETTA
See page 26
If you only visit one place in Malta it must be Valletta. This alluring Baroque capital is home to the country's major museums, besides stunning architecture, lush gardens, lavish churches, hip bars and restaurants, and remnants of a unique local culture.

∨ ĦAĠAR QIM AND MNAJDRA TEMPLE COMPLEX
See page 99
The beauty of these two spectacular Neolithic temples is enhanced by their location on a cliff head overlooking the sea and the untouched Maltese countryside.

< BIRGU
See page 46
Beautiful Birgu offers a pleasant juxtaposition between enormous imposing fortifications, atmospheric old town, and luxury yacht marina.

> THE BLUE LAGOON, COMINO
See page 122
A swath of crystal clear turquoise waters surrounded by wild countryside on a mostly deserted island – these are the things perfect summer afternoons (and photos) are made of. Join a day cruise destined for Comino to best admire Malta's expanses of rocky coastline and cliffs.

< **MDINA**

See page 64

Visitors are swept back in time in the marvellous medieval city of Mdina, where charming winding alleys have kept modernity at bay.

∨ **ḤAL SAFLIENI HYPOGEUM**

See page 95

The stirring and mysterious atmosphere of this stunningly preserved 3600 BCE underground temple complex – a UNESCO World Heritage Site older than Egypt's pyramids or Stonehenge – can not be overstated.

∧ DWEJRA, GOZO
See page 118
Though its most famous landmark – the Azure Window – was lost forever to a winter storm in 2017, Dwejra's Inland Sea and stunning coastal landscape remain must-see's on any Gozo itinerary.

< THE MARSAXLOKK FISH MARKET
See page 101
A chaotic, colourful feast for the senses, the market in this picturesque fishing village is a great place to see – and feast on – local seafood.

∧ FORT ST ELMO & THE NATIONAL WAR MUSEUM
See page 39
This superb new museum – located in a beautifully restored sixteenth-century fort overlooking two harbours – traces the history of military activity in Malta from the Great Siege of 1565 to WWII.

∨ SLIEMA & ST JULIAN'S PROMENADE
See page 54
For a taste of local life, take a stroll (or a dip) along the pretty seaside promenade in cosmopolitan Sliema and St Julian's.

∧ THE BLUE GROTTO, MALTA
See page 100
A dramatic, naturally formed buttress shelters a huge domed cave known for its deep-blue luminous waters.

< ST JOHN'S CO-CATHEDRAL
See page 33
Commissioned by Grand Master Jean de la Cassière and designed by Girolamo Cassar, this opulent building is dedicated to the Order's patron saint, John the Baptist.

< **MALTA AT WAR MUSEUM**
See page 47
The star attraction of this lovely little museum in Birgu is an underground labrinyth of rock-cut World War II shelters.

∨ **GĦAJN TUFFIEĦA BEACH**
See page 90
This large sandy cove, sheltered by blue clay hills, is a favourite amongst locals hiking, sunbathing and swimming. A Knight's-era coastal tower adds historic interest to Malta's most naturally beautiful beach.

A day in Valletta

City Gate. See page 32. Designed by renowned architect Renzo Piano, this is the main entrance to Valletta, flanked by Malta's parliament building. Nearby you'll find Teatru Rjal: an open-air theatre (also designed by Piano) set amidst the ruins of Valletta' Royal Theatre (destroyed by bombs during World War II).

St John's Co-Cathedral. See page 33. This impressive church is the burial place for most of the Grand Masters of the Knights of St John. Breeze through the Cathedral Museum to see the Caravaggio masterpieces.

Museum of Archaeology. See page 33. This sixteenth-century palazzo is home to the priceless artefacts recovered from Malta's ancient Neolithic temples, including the immense "Fat Lady" sculptures.

Lunch. See page 42. Soak up the city's atmosphere at *Caffe Cordina* (and rub shoulders with its politicians) in the café's lavish interior or pretty *pjazza*.

The Grand Master's Palace. See page 35. The centre of political power from the Knights' era to today dominates the city's main square.

Fort St Elmo & The National War Museum. See page 39. The site of the most violent battles of the Great Siege, Fort St Elmo is now home to the National War Museum, offering a superb overview of Malta's history.

Barrakka Gardens. See page 26. Offering Valletta's best sunset views over the Grand Harbour.

Dinner. See page 43. *Harbour Club* has perhaps some of the best contemporary-meets-local fare in Malta, and stunning harbour views.

Strait Street. See page 37. Valletta's former red light district spans the length of the city, and is today home to lively bars and restaurants.

ITINERARIES

City Gate

Caffe Cordina

A bar on Strait Street

A Day in Gozo & Comino

Coffee. See page 120. The light Italian fare at *Captain Spriss* will keep you energised for a day of sightseeing.

The Ċittadella. See page 106. Beautifully preserved, this ancient citadel offers 360-degree views of Gozo's terraced hills and an excellent (free) interpretation centre. See the Cathedral, but skip the museums – Gozo's real attraction lies in its natural beauty, which you'll need the rest of the day to soak in.

Bus Dwejra #311 > Victoria Bus #301 > Mġarr

Xlendi. See page 110. A small, extremely picturesque seaside village with turquoise waters sheltered by striking limestone cliffs, with a seaside promenade lined by excellent restaurants.

🍴 **Lunch.** See page 121. The most relaxing restaurant in Xlendi, *Zafiro* specialises in homemade pasta, fresh seafood and lovely sea views.

Xlendi Bus #306 or 330 > Bus Victoria #311 > Dwejra

Dwejra and the Inland Sea. See page 118. Once home to Malta's natural wonder, the Azure Window (until it fell in to the sea in 2017), Dwejra's attraction persists in its wildly beautiful coastal landscape and Inland Sea.

Dbieġi Crafts Village. See page 119. Pick up souvenirs for better prices than in Malta, including Maltese lace, local sheep's wool sweaters, silver filigree jewellery and handmade leather goods and ceramics

Victoria Bus #307 or 322 > Xagħra

Ġgantija temples. See page 112. Gozo's own Neolithic wonder, Ġgantija temples are also one of the oldest free-standing structures in human history, pre-dating Stonehenge and Egypt's pyramids.

Xagħra Bus #307 or 322 > Victoria

Ċittadella

Xlendi

Dwejra and The Inland Sea

Malta for Families

Popeye's Village. See page 89. The set for the 1980's Robin Williams movie is preserved as a small but quaint seaside family fun park.

Mellieħa Bus #101 > Ghadira Beach, Mellieħa Bus #221 > Qawra

National Aquarium. See page 82. Get to know the fish you'll encounter while swimming in Malta, as well as a host of tropical visitors including clownfish, rays and tiny sharks.

Lunch. See page 91. *Acqua Marina* is a hidden gem, run by a gracious family, offering simple, authentic, undeniably good Sicilian cuisine.

Bugibba Bus #48 > Floriana Bus #3 > Kalkara

Esplora. See page 52. Malta's National Science Museum, housed in a former British Navy hospital in the Grand Harbour, hosts over 200 delightful interactive exhibits and a planetarium that appears to levitate within the shell of a WWII damaged palace.

Birgu Bus #1-4 > Valletta Bus #13, 14 or 16 > Sliema

Dinner. See page 62. Fill up on *Piccolo Padre*'s wood-fired pizzas and generous plates of pasta at this charming, family-friendly seaside restaurant, a local institution.

Evening stroll. See page 54. Along the pretty 5km promenade that stretches from Sliema to St Julian's.

Popeye's Village

National Aquarium

Esplora

Military Malta

Fort St Angelo. See page 50. Fort St Angelo's recently restored, tremendously thick fortifications plunge directly into the sea and embody the intimidating military spirit of the Knights.

Fort Rinella. See page 52. Home to a truly massive 100-tonne gun, this volunteer-run fort also offers delightful historic cavalry demonstrations where gentle, retired race horses steal the show.

Valletta fortifications. See page 26. Stroll along Valletta's seashore for an invader's view of its imposing fortifications. A well worn path begins as you descend the stairs opposite the Sacra Infermeria and ends at the Valletta-Sliema ferry.

Lascaris War Rooms. See page 30. With guided tours offered by kind and knowledgeable volunteers, the Lascaris War Rooms were the secret setting for Malta's disproportionately important role in WWII.

Palace Armoury. See page 35. When the Knights departed Malta, they left behind a rich cultural legacy – plus an impressive cache of sixteenth-century armour.

Fort St Angelo

Lascaris War Rooms

Palace Armoury

Baroque Malta

Grand Master's Palace State Rooms. See page 35. One of the first buildings constructed in Valletta by Grand Master Jean de Vallette in 1566 after his victory in the Great Siege.

St John's Co-Cathedral. See page 33. A dizzying expression of Baroque extravagance. No surface is left untouched by gilding, painting, marble or sculpture. Also home to several of Baroque master Caravaggio's best works.

Mdina Cathedral. See page 67. More restrained than its sister cathedral, St John's, Mdina's Cathedral is nonetheless impressive and dominates the skyline for miles around.

Maltese balconies. Look up in nearly every street to be rewarded with views of Malta's charming wooden balconies, believed to be inspired by the Grand Master's Palace's first extravagant examples.

Teatru Manoel. See page 37. Like Malta itself – Teatru Manoel is small but stunning. Take a 30-minute guided tour (€5) or visit during a scheduled performance (tickets from €10).

Grand Master's Palace State Rooms

St John's Co-Cathedral Museum

Maltese balconies

Ancient Malta

Ħaġar Qim and Mnajdra temples. See page 99. These two striking Neolithic temples (older than Egypt's pyramids) sit amongst untouched Maltese countryside. A compelling interpretation centre attempts to unravel their mysteries.

Tarxien Temples. See page 94. Nestled amongst residential townhouses, this complex of four megalithic structures dates back to 3600 BCE and is home to some of the best surviving examples of prehistoric art.

Tarxien Temples

Ħal Saflieni Hypogeum. See page 95. Carved into solid limestone over 6000 years ago, this haunting, beautiful and mysterious underground burial site is not to be missed.

Cart ruts. See page 77. An abundance of ancient, parallel ruts gouged into the limestone surface that lead, inexplicably, off of cliffs or abruptly end; their use is as yet unknown, which adds to their allure.

National Museum of Archaeology. See page 33. A sixteenth-century palazzo home to the bulk of Malta's ancient treasures, this museum provides an overview of the country's ancient history from 5200 to 2500 BCE through artefacts and scholarship.

National Museum of Archaeology

Ġgantija temples. See page 112. The oldest temples found in the country, local legend holds that this temple was built by a race of giants (not so far-fetched, when you see their size).

Ġgantija temples

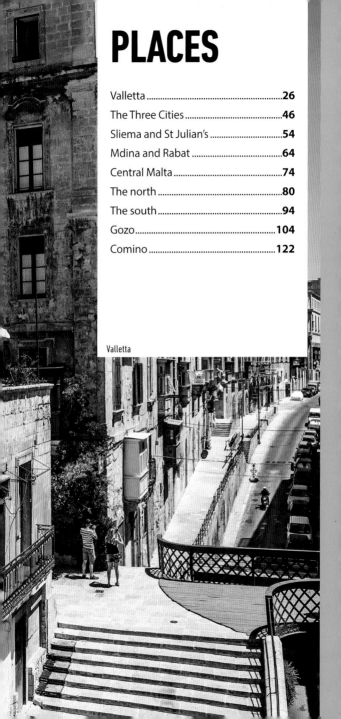

PLACES

Valletta

Valletta

Few leave Valletta (commonly referred to as il-Belt or The City) without falling in love with this tiny capital city, designated in its entirety as a UNESCO World Heritage site and 2018's European Capital of Culture. Valletta – one of Europe's first planned cities – was an impenetrable Baroque capital that is now the centre of Malta's cultural, culinary and commercial life. Immerse yourself in its layers of history, from the late Renaissance to the contemporary, as you scale its many levels – for this is a city of staircases, built unusually short and deep to accommodate the armour-bearing Knights of St John, while a ring of golden limestone fortifications encloses its tight grid of narrow streets full of churches, palaces and townhouses. The outstanding cathedral and Knights' former palace head a list of sights that include Malta's national museums and art galleries. Valletta is also home to a blooming bar and foodie scene.

Auberge de Castille

MAP P.28, POCKET MAP E7
Pjazza Kastilja. Closed to the public.
Dominating Valletta's highest point, the **Auberge de Castille** is the largest and most impressive of Valletta's four surviving *auberges* (historic inns for regional groups of Knights). This monumental Baroque building stands as a reminder of the superiority of the Knights of Castille, one of the brotherhood's largest chapters. Though designed in the 1570s by Girolamo Cassar in the austere style the Knights then preferred, it was rebuilt in grand Baroque style during the eighteenth century to occupy a whole block. The large column-framed doorway is topped with a bust of Grand Master de Fonseca, who initiated the rebuilding. Today, the Auberge de Castille houses the prime minister's office and isn't open to the public, but with two imposing cannon flanking its front door, it's a popular stop for photo opportunities. Linger here long enough and you may even spot a dignitary or two.

Saluting Battery

Upper Barrakka Gardens and the Saluting Battery

MAP P.28, POCKET MAP E7
Pjazza Kastilja. Daily 7.30am–10pm. Free.
Set high behind the ramparts of Valletta's fortifications, this small garden, sprinkled with fragrant

Visiting Valletta

All **buses** to and from Valletta terminate at the bus station outside its main gate. If you're **driving**, avoid entering the city, which is Malta's only controlled vehicle access (CVA) area. An access levy is charged (rental car companies often add their own processing fees to this) and parking is limited – you can avoid the CVA by parking in the multi-storey car park near the bus station (prices vary depending on time, averaging €2/hr). Alternately, use the **park-and-ride service** (€0.40); the car park, signposted in major approaches to Valletta, is just outside Floriana, and free mini-buses shuttle commuters between here and Valletta's St George's Square, Auberge de Castille or Fort St Elmo every few minutes 6am–9pm. From Sliema, a **ferry** makes the 5min journey to Marsamxett on the western flank of Valletta (daily every 30min: June–Oct 7am–midnight; Nov–May 7am–7pm) and a second ferry travels from Valletta's Barriera Wharf to Birgu (daily every 30min: June–Oct 6.30am–11.30pm; Nov–May 6.30am–7pm). Each costs €1.50 single or €2.80 return, €1.75 single or €3.30 return after 7.30pm.

There is one infrequent **circular public bus service** inside Valletta's walls (€1.50 winter, €2 summer), but the city is small enough to see **on foot**. There are also small **electric mini cabs** (akin to golf karts), which operate from 8am to 8pm; flag one down as they pass by or visit the mini cab stand in front of St John's Co-Cathedral (maximum fare €5 per trip, or €8 from the city to the cruise ship terminal). Next Bike, a private **bike rental system**, also has several bicycle stands in Valletta but the city's dramatic hills make it difficult to traverse on two wheels (registration required; €1.50/30min plus €1 for each additional 30min or €16/day).

flowerbeds, was created in 1661 by the Italian knight Flaminio Balbiani as a retreat for the Knights. Much of it, including its arcaded section, is the original design (the arcaded section was originally roofed, but when Grand Master Ximenes de Texada discovered that dissident Knights were meeting here in 1775 to plot against him, he ordered the roof stripped off as a symbolic warning). The garden still provides a refuge from city bustle and summer heat, but the main reason to visit is for the panoramic view from Valletta's highest point: a vista taking in the breadth of the **Grand Harbour**, including the fantastic medieval townscapes and fortifications of the **Three Cities** (see page 46).

The **Saluting Battery**, accessed from within the garden, spreads over a series of chambers that once served as ammunition stores (daily 10am–5pm; ☎ 2180 0992; €3). Today it holds a display of weaponry from the three hundred years it served as an artillery battery for protecting the Grand Harbour, including an anti-aircraft gun that was installed on the terrace in World War II. For history buffs, guided tours are offered on the hour (included in your entrance fee), and two films are shown in rotation: one on the history of "timeguns", and another about the history of the Saluting Battery. At noon and 4pm every day a cannon is fired as a salute – resurrecting a practice dating from the British period.

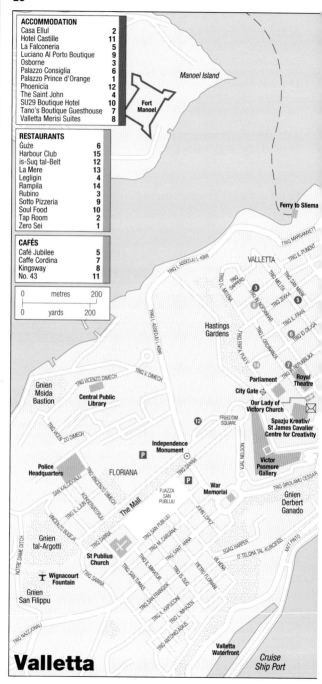

ACCOMMODATION

Casa Ellul	2
Hotel Castille	11
La Falconeria	5
Luciano Al Porto Boutique	9
Osborne	3
Palazzo Consiglia	6
Palazzo Prince d'Orange	1
Phoenicia	12
The Saint John	4
SU29 Boutique Hotel	10
Tano's Boutique Guesthouse	7
Valletta Merisi Suites	8

RESTAURANTS

Gúze	6
Harbour Club	15
is-Suq tal-Belt	12
La Mere	13
Legligin	4
Rampila	14
Rubino	3
Sotto Pizzeria	9
Soul Food	10
Tap Room	2
Zero Sei	1

CAFÉS

Café Jubilee	5
Caffe Cordina	7
Kingsway	8
No. 43	11

Valletta

BARS	
Alchemy	1
Bridge Bar	9
Café Society	8
Charles Grech	7
Loop	2
The Pub	4
Trabuxu	6
Wild Honey	3
Yard 32	5

SHOPS	
Cek Cik	10
Charles & Ron	3
Kir Royal	9
Marquis de Vissac	6
Meli Book Shop	5
Mint Sparrow	8
No.Me	1
Que	4
Theobroma Cacao Collective	2
White Shop	7

Marsamxett Harbour

St Elmo Bay

Fort St Elmo

TRIQ MARSAMXETT

ST CHRISTOPHER'S STREET

SAN BASTJAN

GENDUS

IL-MANDRAGG

TRIQ L'ISPALJAR L'QADIM

ST ELMO PLACE

ST ELMO PLACE

The National War Museum

MISRAH L-INDIPENDENZA

TRIQ L-ARCISQOF

TRIQ ZEKKA

TRIQ IL-FRAN

TRIQ D'OEJDA

ST NICHOLAS STREET

TRIQ SAN DUMINKU

Basilica of Our Lady of Mount Carmel

Manoel Theatre

TRIQ TEATRU L-QADIM

TRIQ IR-REPUBBLIKA

Casa Rocca Piccola

The Malta Experience

BLITZ

MISRAH SAN GORG

Grand Master's Palace & Armoury

TRIQ IL-MERKANTI

Jesuit Church

TRIQ SAN PAWL

TRIQ SANT ORSLA

TRIQ IL-MEDITERRAN

TRIQ S. LUCIA

MISRAH IR-REPUBBLIKA

TRIQ SAN GWANN

Malta Contemporary Art

TRIQ SAN FELIĊ

National Museum of Archaeology

MISRAH SAN GWANN

St John's Co-Cathedral & Museum

St Paul's Shipwreck Church

LVANT

Lower Barakka Gardens

Siege Bell Monument

TRIQ MELITA

TRIQ IL-MERKANTI

MUŻA

ST BARBARA BASTION

XATT IL-BARRIERA

Auberge de Castille

PJAZZA KASTILJA

Lascaris War Rooms

Upper Barakka Gardens

Saluting Battery

XATT LASCARIS

N

Grand Harbour

Fort St Angelo

XATT IL-FORN

Birgu

Gardjola Gardens

PORTU SALVU

TRIQ IS-SIRENA

XATT JUAN B. AZOPARDO

TRIQ IL-GRIĊA

TRIQ MONTE...

VITTORIOSA

San Filippu

Dockyard Creek

Lascaris War Rooms

MAP P.28, POCKET MAP E7
Lascaris Ditch; entry either from
Girolamo Cassar St or San Anton St
(from the latter, follow signs from
outside Upper Barakka Gardens) ☎ 2123
4717, ⊕ lascariswarrooms.com. Daily
10am–5pm. Adults €12, children €5.

This fascinating (albeit damp)
underground complex, gouged deep
into the bedrock, was originally
used by the Knights as living
quarters for their slaves. In 1940,
it was converted into the **Lascaris
War Rooms**, the British forces'
Maltese centre of operations and
the headquarters of the Royal
Navy's Mediterranean Fleet during
World War II. Conditions were
claustrophobic – a thousand
people worked here, 240 at a
time in six-hour shifts – but it
was from Lascaris that the Allies
changed the course of World
War II in the Mediterranean by
severely disrupting the Axis supplies
to North Africa, launching the
invasion of Sicily, and eventually
engineering Italy's surrender. An
interesting **museum** now re-creates
the wartime atmosphere with
wax dummies, maps, props and
examples of weaponry such as the
J-type Contact Mines that the
Italians planted around Malta's seas.
Each room is dedicated to an area of
operation; the largest concentrates
on Operation Husky, the 1943
Allied invasion of Sicily directed by
General Dwight Eisenhower, where
a large map of Sicily details the
multi-pronged attack by air and sea.
A **short film** on Malta's wartime
experience is shown throughout

Valletta's renaissance

Visitors may notice an unusual number of **abandoned buildings** in
the capital city. In fact, about thirty percent of property is vacant and
much of this uninhabitable. During World War II, Valletta sustained
heavy damage from aerial bombardments, and then changing
social and economic conditions (including the departure of the
British navy and most of the city's jobs in the 1960s) led to a mass
exodus from the city and, eventually, the whole country. Post-World
War II, Valletta earned a reputation for being derelict and unsafe,
with most residents living in government-subsidized housing. To put
things in perspective, during World War II the city's population was
over 23,000 but by 2015 it had plummeted to 6000 (of which more
than 25 percent were over 65). Despite this (temporary) decline, in
1980 Valletta was named a UNESCO World Heritage Site as an ideal
example of a late Renaissance planned city and its association with
the Knights, one of the greatest military forces of modern Europe.

Today, Valletta is undergoing a rapid renaissance. Bars,
restaurants, shops and hotels breathed new life into the city for its
2018 European Capital of Culture title. Streets are pedestrianised,
public squares completely regenerated and new cultural
institutions like MUŻA (see page 32) and the Valletta Design
Cluster (see page 36) have thrown open their doors. Gradually,
younger residents are returning to the city and record numbers
of tourists and cruise passengers are discovering its charms.
Derelict buildings are fewer, and real estate prices are skyrocketing
in anticipation of the city's complete regeneration. It will be some
time before the entire city bustles with life once more, but the tide
is turning: Valletta has never been lovelier, with an eclectic blend of
new and old at every turn. This is the perfect time to visit.

the day, and an hour underground here gives a good impression of what life must have been like during this tumultuous time. If you have the opportunity, a **tour** with one of the museum's charming volunteer guides is worthwhile. Recommended viewing before your visit is *The Malta Story,* a 1950s World War II movie filmed in the Lascaris War Rooms a few years after operations here ceased.

Victor Pasmore Gallery

MAP P.28, POCKET MAP E7
The Polverista, St James Counterguard, Annexe of the Central Bank of Malta ☎ 2550 0000, ⓦ victorpasmoregallery. com. Mon–Fri 11am–3pm. Free.
Located in a *polverista* or gunpowder magazine built during the construction of the outer fortification walls of Valletta in the 1640s, the **Victor Pasmore Gallery** features a compact but compelling permanent display of works by British abstract artist Victor Pasmore (1908–98), many produced after his move to the island in 1966.

Spazju Kreattiv/St James Cavalier Centre for Creativity

MAP P.28, POCKET MAP E7
Castille Square ☎ 2122 3200, ⓦ kreattivita. org. Mon–Fri 9am–1pm, Sat & Sun 10am–1pm. Free.
Malta's national centre for modern arts occupies the historic site of **St James Cavalier**, an imposing pentagonal tower built opposite the Auberge de Castille in the 1570s to serve as a rearguard defence position. Within its thick walls sit a series of half-barrel ammunition chambers connected to a ramp that leads to the roof (where heavy guns used to be installed). The complex was converted into an arts centre in 1995 by Richard England, Malta's most famous contemporary architect, and the eleven former ammunition chambers now stage temporary art exhibitions in all media by Maltese and international

Victor Pasmore Gallery

artists. A small **cinema** screens a rotation of independent films and live opera performances (check the website for schedules). On weekends between October and May, plays, musicals and dance events are also staged in its **theatre-in-the-round**.

Hastings Gardens

MAP P.28, POCKET MAP D7
Triq Papa Piju V. Daily 7.30am–dusk. Free.
Set behind Valletta's fortifications, **Hastings Garden** is dedicated to Lord Hastings, a former British governor who died at sea in 1827 and is buried in the Neoclassical shrine at its centre. The garden's small oaks, pines and shrubs lack appeal, but its lofty viewpoints are reason enough to visit (especially at sunset) – you can see how the Floriana Line fortifications fold over each other to give a 180-degree fire-range; in the moat below, more than a few Hollywood movies have been filmed. Further in the distance, you'll spot Marsamxett Harbour with its yacht marinas, then Manoel Island with its pretty fort and the skylines of urban Sliema and St Julian's. In July, a weekend-long **wine festival**

Parliament

sees this garden come alive with music, local varietals and thirsty crowds (see page 147).

City Gate, Parliament and Royal Theatre

MAP P.28, POCKET MAP E7

The area surrounding Valletta's main entrance, **City Gate**, is proof that Valletta is not a city frozen in time. Designed in 2013 by renowned architect Renzo Piano (famous for the Shard in London and Paris' Centre Pompidou), the sleek and minimalist City Gate comprises a footbridge that crosses an 18m-deep dry moat and passes through the city's ramparts. Entering the city, visitors are confronted with a sweeping view of Malta's Parliament buildings – designed by Piano to appear to levitate above the public square below – and the city's main thoroughfare, **Republic Street**. Both the City Gate and Parliament were constructed entirely of cream-coloured limestone blocks painstakingly installed in the exact order they were extracted from quarries in Gozo – note the delicate pink veins that run across the facade as a result. The innovative design of the **Parliament**'s facade is intended to filter solar radiation while filling the building with natural light,

reducing the structure's energy footprint. Adjacent, you'll find **Pjazza Teatru Rjal** (the Royal Theatre; ⓦ pjazzateatrurjal.com), where Piano designed a splendid modern open-air theatre within the ruins of the Royal Opera, a lavish nineteenth-century theatre decimated by World War II bombings. During the summer months, Pjazza Teatru Rjal is an enchanting venue for cultural performances and cinema screenings under the stars (check the website for listings).

MUŻA

MAP P.28, POCKET MAP E7
Merchant St, Auberge d'Italie ⓣ 2122 1047, ⓦ muza.heritagemalta.org.

MUŻA (*Mużew Nazzjonali tal-Arti*) is Malta's national museum of art, located in the **Auberge d'Italie** on Merchant Street. The building was the seat of the Italian Knights of the Order of St John. MUŻA is due to open in 2018 to replace the old Fine Arts Museum (South Street, Valletta). A completely refurbished space three times larger than its predecessor, MUŻA houses an expanded permanent collection of artefacts and works of art, including 120 new acquisitions from local artists, following four themes: the Mediterranean, Europe, Empire and Artist.

Our Lady of Victory Church

MAP P.28, POCKET MAP E7

Triq in-Nofsinhar, Victory Square. Mon–Fri 8.30am–3.30pm. €4 including audioguide and museum.

The first church built in Valletta, the tiny **Our Lady of Victory** was erected to mark the spot where the foundation stone of the city was laid by Grand Master Jean de Valette in 1566. The titular painting behind the main altar, depicting the birth of the Virgin Mary, is said to date to the same period. According to his wishes, La Valette was originally buried here and his coats of arms were painted inside the church. His remains were later transferred to **St John's Co-Cathedral**.

National Museum of Archaeology

MAP P.28, POCKET MAP E7

Republic St ☏ 2122 1623, ⊕ heritagemalta. org. Daily: Jan & Feb 9am–7pm; March–Dec 9am–6pm. €5 including audioguide.

Built in 1575 to a design by Girolamo Cassar, the former Auberge de Provence now houses the **National Museum of Archaeology**, with an array of exhibits dating from 5200 to 2500 BCE that represent the legacy of the Neolithic era's most advanced nation. Though the display cases themselves could benefit from a modern facelift, it is well worth spending some time here to learn about the enormity of this little island's ancient history. The sheer size and age of the artefacts here will also hold interest for children.

The collection is exhibited chronologically, starting from 5200–4400 BCE with skeletal remains and some of the earliest artistic representations of humans. The exhibits then describe the discovery of Malta's various **Neolithic temples**, offering theories on how these massive complexes were constructed. There's even a stone model dating

from the temple-building period, considered to be the first ever architectural design. The most stirring displays are in the **Human Figure** room, including phallic stone symbols and a cluster of voluptuous female nudes and sexless figures with pleated skirts and headdresses thought to have been made for ceremonial use. Some of the figures are headless, suggesting that different heads were affixed to the loop at the neck for different ceremonies. The museum's star exhibit, the "**sleeping lady**", is a delicate, hand-sized figurine unearthed from the Hypogeum that depicts a large woman reclining on a couch; carved in minute detail, her body's tranquil pose could be at temporary or eternal rest. The Neolithic floor ends with the dramatic Tarxien Hall, where contents of the 4200-square-metre **Tarxien Temple complex** are exhibited, including megaliths carved with animals, fish and spiral motifs (thought to symbolize a worldview of cyclical continuity) and, more importantly, hollowed altars in which animal bones and flint knives were found – the strongest evidence of animal sacrifices in Malta's temples.

On the upper floor, separate exhibits on **Bronze Age** and **Phoenician** artefacts present mostly pottery and funerary art, with an interesting section dedicated to Malta's **cart ruts** (see page 7). The remainder of the upper floor comprises several ornate and elaborately decorated palace rooms that house temporary exhibitions.

St John's Co-Cathedral and Museum

MAP P.28, POCKET MAP E7

St John St ☏ 2122 0536, ⊕ stjohnsco cathedral.com. Mon–Fri 9.30am–4.30pm, Sat 9.30am–12.30pm. €10 including audioguide.

Don't let its austere facade fool you – stepping inside **St John's Co-Cathedral** is like entering a brilliant jewellery box. The Cathedral was designed by Girolamo Cassar in 1570 as the conventual church of the Order, replacing St Lawrence Church in Birgu (see page 49). In the latter half of the seventeenth century the Knights set about transforming the plain interior of the cathedral – dedicated to the Order's patron saint – into a blaze of Baroque art. The Calabrian artist Mattia Preti (1613–99) supervised the twenty-year project, which in some years cost more than Malta's entire military budget. Most of the artworks in the cavernous nave are the work of Preti, who was also responsible for several of the altar paintings.

The **nave** of the cathedral is overwhelmingly sumptuous. Pillars are ablaze with mesmerizing gold and blue leaf carvings and representations of the Maltese Cross, while the eighteen vignettes on the vault, depicting episodes from St John's life, took Preti five years to complete (painting directly onto the concave ceiling, he had to tinker carefully with the perspective so that the view from the ground wouldn't be distorted). The floor of the nave, meanwhile, has 364 inlaid marble tombs of influential Knights: each features a Latin eulogy and epitaph framed by symbols of prestige and glory.

The artistic diversity of the Co-Cathedral was further enhanced when **eight side-chapels** were individually assigned to each *langue*, or Knightly regional grouping, which competed to create the most flamboyant decoration (you'd be hard pressed to pick a winner, though the Chapel of the Langue of Aragon would certainly be in the running). To the right of the chancel in the chapel dedicated to Our Lady of Carafa, Grand Master La Vallette is interred in a stone sarcophagus; this is the only part of the church that retains its original monastic simplicity (La Vallette would have been pleased).

Departing the nave, visitors enter the **Oratory of St John**, which holds the cathedral's most valuable relic: the *Beheading of St John the Baptist*, **Caravaggio**'s magnificent masterpiece painted in 1608. A stunning achievement for its time, many art historians consider it the best painting of the seventeenth century given its grim realism, excellent composition and virtuoso use of light and shade. The second Caravaggio on display, *St Jerome Writing*, is a less dramatic but deeply human work. The oratory itself – full of dense carvings and motifs – is also the work of Preti.

Beyond the oratory, a **museum** showcases the church's moveable art: heaps of silverware and vestments, various portraits of Knights and three huge and majestic Flemish tapestries dating from 1702 (these were formerly hung in the Co-Cathedral's nave). By the time you read this, the museum will have completed a total refurbishment and extension project to accommodate increasing visitor numbers – expect even more opulence on display. Note that high heels are banned in the interest of preserving the nave's intricate tombs (slippers can be purchased at €1.20 per pair). Women must cover their shoulders (free shawls are provided) and visitor numbers are limited to 52 persons in the Oratory at a time.

St Paul's Shipwreck Church

MAP P.28, POCKET MAP E7
St Paul St ☎ 2123 6013. Daily 9.30am–noon & 4–6pm. Free.

The capital's most opulent church after the Co-Cathedral, **St Paul's** is dedicated to the shipwreck of Malta's favourite saint in 60 AD (see page 148). The present structure, consecrated in 1740, is the third incarnation on this site and its rich and dense interior is awash in crimson and gold. Closer inspection reveals silver chandeliers and statues of the Apostles, ornate altars in the side-chapels, and numerous memorials to St Paul including a fragment of the saint's wrist bone set in a gilded reliquary and the pillar on which he was beheaded. This church celebrates its feast twice a year (Feb 10 and June 29, both public holidays) with lively, elaborate parades.

St George's Square

MAP P.28, POCKET MAP E6
Republic St

Valletta's main square, flanked by the Grand Master's Palace and an Italian Cultural Institute, is the site for most of Malta's national celebrations and events, including Carnival, New Year's Eve, Malta Arts Festival (ⓦ maltaartsfestival.org) and Malta Fashion Week (ⓦ fashionweek.com. mt). The fountain puts on a musical show hourly throughout the day, set against the regal *Malta Suite* score by composer Charles Camilleri. A monument here commemorates the events of Sette Giugno (June 7, 1919), when British troops fired into a crowd of people protesting increasing living costs in this square, killing four.

Summer nights in St George's Square are particularly lovely, as locals pour into the square to escape the heat of their flats and children splash about in the fountain. Passing through the square, take note of the impressive green balconies that wrap around the corners of the Grand Master's Palace – these are thought to be the inspiration for many of the ubiquitous Maltese balconies of today.

Grand Master's Palace and Armoury

MAP P.28, POCKET MAP E7
Republic St, St George's Square ☎ 2124 9349, ⓦ heritagemalta.org. **Daily 9am–5pm. €10.**

An imposing two-storey building occupying an entire block, the **Grand Master's Palace** served as Malta's seat of political power from 1571, when it was designed by

Girolamo Cassar for the Knights, to 2015, when Parliament was moved to its new home designed by Renzo Piano (see page 32). Today, it is home to the Office of the President of Malta and five of its grand rooms are open for the public to explore. Perhaps the most compelling part of the palace is the handsome corridor that connects these rooms, richly decorated with marble floors depicting the Grand Master's coats of arms and painted from floor to ceiling with a series of lunettes depicting knightly naval battles. Adjoining State Rooms feature dramatic, thick-coffered and panelled timber ceilings with gilding, massive chandeliers and portraits of various Grand Masters (who each modified and embellished the palace during their tenure).

The **Throne Room** was used by Grand Masters to host ambassadors and high ranking dignitaries; the President of Malta continues to use the room for the same purpose today. The frescoes in this room were painted by 1576 by the Italian Matteo Perez D'Aleccio and depict key events of the Knights' history. The **Council Room** (where the ruling council, akin

St George's Square during Malta's initiation as European Capital of Culture 2018

to today's government cabinet, held its meetings) is adorned with three-hundred-year-old copies of the fantastic Gobelin Tapestries, depicting romanticized scenes of New World animals and hunters encountered by the German Prince Johan Mauritz of Nassau during his expedition from 1636 to 1644. The **State Dining Room**, rebuilt after being hit during a World War II air raid, features portraits of Maltese Heads of State since the country achieved its independence in 1964. The **Page's Waiting Room** is connected to the Grand Master's private apartments (disappointingly, not open to the public) and the frescoes here describe scenes from the Knights' history before they arrived in Malta. In the adjoining and richly crimson **Hall of Ambassadors** the fresco series continues, with the addition of Baroque portraits of Grand Masters.

On the ground floor, the absorbing **Palace Armoury** was opened to the public in 1860 as Malta's first public museum. One of the world's largest collections and the most visible and tangible symbol of the order's military glories, the armoury spreads over two barrel-vaulted halls that were originally used as the

palace stables. The first room now displays armour and the second a mass of weaponry, including swords, muskets, cannons and crossbows. The Knights had enough military hardware to equip an army of 18,000 and although only a fraction of this haul remains, the 5000 or so pieces on display are representative of virtually the whole range of armaments produced between the sixteenth and eighteenth centuries in Malta and other European countries. The highlight of the Armoury is undoubtedly the priceless damascened suit of body armour that belonged to Grand Master Wignacourt, entirely encrusted in gold and silver fleur-de-lys and military symbols.

Il-Mandraġġ

MAP P.28, POCKET MAP F6

Occupying the northern corner of Valletta, the former slum district of **Il-Mandraġġ** is demarcated on two sides by the sea, and on the other two by Old Theatre Street and Strait Street. Until the 1960s, the area's alleys were densely populated and alive with the activity of blacksmiths, butchers, bakers and bars. Il-Mandraġġ was described in the 1930s by British writer Evelyn Waugh as "the most concentrated and intense slum in the world." This sentiment, unfortunately, has persisted locally, giving il-Mandraġġ a reputation as a rough and dangerous area. Today, the reality is quite the opposite. Crumbling stone buildings towering over narrow alleys remain faithful to the original urban fabric of Valletta, and are slowly being regenerated into refurbished flats, artist studios and boutique hotels. Malta's national design centre, the **Valletta Design Cluster**, is also located here.

It's worth exploring this rapidly changing area to absorb the atmosphere of the "real" Valletta (*il-Belt*) that lies beyond the city's pristine palazzos. The area is safe, and scratching the surface reveals

Manoel Theatre

a close-knit community who are "Beltin first, Maltese second." If you really want to step off the beaten path, descend through the **Jew's Sally Port** at the end of St Nicholas Street for a taste of local life; here, fighting for space on the seashore, you'll find a concentration of tumbledown shanties where families gather on hot summer evenings for languid barbeques.

The Gut

MAP P.28, POCKET MAP E7

This narrow section of lower Strait Street, nicknamed "**The Gut**" by British sailors, is Valletta's former red light district. For virtually all of Valletta's history, the area was populated with a combination of small bars, taverns, music halls and brothels, but its heyday was from the 1920s to the 1960s when prostitutes, drag queens and jazz musicians entertained British and American sailors here. Independence in 1964 caused a steep decline in the number of visiting servicemen, and from the 1970s most of Strait Street closed down, to be abandoned and unloved for the next forty years. The awarding to Valletta of the 2018 European Capital of Culture title sparked a renewed interest in the area and today The Gut is at the centre of Malta's most exciting bar and restaurant scene, with several establishments, such as *Alchemy* (see page 44), restored to their former glory. As you wander along this narrow alley, look for the **original signs** for bars and music halls, miraculously still in situ. Most food and drink establishments are located at the intersection of Strait Street and Old Theatre Street, though *Yard 32* (see page 45) and *Trabuxu* (see page 45) – located in the historically more gentrified area of upper Strait Street, which was frequented by more senior Navy officers – are also worth seeking out. On weekends during the summer, live musicians perform up and down the street.

Manoel Theatre

MAP P.28, POCKET MAP E6
115 Old Theatre St ☎ 2122 2618, ⊛ teatru manoel.com.mt. Open for tours Mon–Fri 10am–4.30pm, Sat 10am–12.30pm. Tours every 45min; €5 including audioguide.

Malta's national theatre and home of the Malta Philharmonic Orchestra, the **Manoel Theatre** (Teatru Manoel) is one of Europe's oldest and most impressive. Personally funded by Grand Master Antonio Manoel de Vilhena in 1731 "for the honest recreation of the people" (which phrase is inscribed above the main entrance to the theatre), it is wholly built from timber with an intimate six-hundred-seat oval-shaped interior ringed by boxes, topped by an elegant pale-blue-and-gold trompe l'oeil ceiling. Two reservoirs underground perfect the acoustics, which are so precise that orchestral conductors have to work from one side of the stage to prevent the rustle made by turning the pages of music sheets being audible in the auditorium. Half-hour **guided tours** outline the construction of the theatre and its history, but the Manoel is best appreciated during evening performances (see page 142).

Basilica of Our Lady of Mount Carmel

MAP P.28, POCKET MAP E6
Old Theatre St. Daily 7am–9pm. Free.

The **Basilica of Our Lady of Mount Carmel**'s looming dome, together with the spire of the nearby **St John's Anglican Cathedral**, are the iconic features of Valletta's skyline. Following its destruction in World War II, the rebuilding of the basilica (the original dated from the 1570s) took twenty years and demonstrated a reassertion of the dominance of Baroque architecture in Malta. The resulting structure shows more concern with size than it does with artistic detail; the interior of the church is uncharacteristically restrained, while the egg-shaped dome attempts to eclipse its neighbour.

Blitz

MAP P.28, POCKET MAP E6
St Lucy St ☎ 2122 4992, ⊛ thisisblitz.com.
Blitz is an independent, not-for-profit contemporary arts project space situated in a four-level, four-hundred-year-old Valletta townhouse. Its unique setting and excellent temporary exhibitions make it worth a visit; check the website for listings.

Casa Rocca Piccola

MAP P.28, POCKET MAP F6
74 Republic St ☎ 2122 1499,
⊛ casaroccapiccola.com. Daily 10am–5pm.
€9 including guided tour.
Casa Rocca Piccola is a private sixteenth-century palazzo owned and operated by a noble Maltese family; their ancestor Cosimo de Piro left Rhodes in the general exodus of the Knights of St John in 1530. The palazzo's current inhabitants, the Marquis Nicholas de Piro and his wife Frances, were the first members of the Maltese aristocracy to open their house to the public, offering visitors a glimpse of what must lie beyond the palatial facades of Valletta's other palazzos. Highlights include an underground cistern turned World War II shelter, a chatty pet parrot named Kiko, and a delightful collection of local contemporary and historic art.

Malta Contemporary Art

MAP P.28, POCKET MAP F7
12 Felix St ☎ 9957 9131,
⊛ maltacontemporaryart.com. Thurs–Sat
10am–noon & 3–6pm. Free.
Founded in 2008, Malta's foremost **contemporary art gallery** hosts an engaging and diverse programme of exhibitions and events. Artists who have exhibited here include Cyprien Gaillard, Simon Starling, Basim Magdy, Anthea Hamilton, Haris Epaminonda and Spartacus Chetwynd. Check the gallery's website for current exhibition listings.

Jesuit Church

MAP P.28, POCKET MAP F7
Merchant St.
The **Jesuit Church** is one of the oldest in Valletta, built between 1592 and 1609 with an originally plain facade that was redesigned by famous Baroque architect Francesco Buonamici in 1647. The interior is uniquely serene by Maltese standards, with a delicate buttery yellow colour and restrained Doric architectural influences. Its oratory invites further exploration, a tiny room with a candy-coloured ceiling and an overwhelming profusion of paintings, sculpture and marble that more than compensate for the restraint of the church proper. The adjacent Jesuit College, built concurrently, is today the **University of Malta's** Valletta campus.

Lower Barrakka Gardens

MAP P.28, POCKET MAP F7
East St. Daily 7.30am–dusk. Free.
Located at the tip of Valletta's peninsula, **Lower Barrakka Gardens** are the counterpoint to their sister, Upper Barrakka (see page 26). Slightly smaller but no less attractive, visitors can admire views from the Grand Harbour here under the shade of olive trees. With a cheerful pub and casual kiosk flanking its entrance, Lower Barrakka Gardens is also a popular meeting place for locals. Enjoy a local lager here while taking in a splendid taste of life in *il-Belt*.

Siege Bell Monument

MAP P.28, POCKET MAP F7
Mediterranean St. Daily 9am–5pm. Free.
This huge **bell**, mounted on a specially built podium, was erected in 1992 and jointly inaugurated by the then Maltese President Ċensu Tabone and Queen Elizabeth II to commemorate the anniversary of the George Cross Award to Malta (see page 39) and to honour the seven thousand servicemen, women and civilians who died here during World War II. The

bell tolls daily at noon, and its boom – intended as a reminder of Malta's war victims – can be heard throughout Valletta. A visit also offers panoramic harbour views.

Fort St Elmo and the National War Museum

MAP P.28, POCKET MAP F6
St Elmo Place ⊙ 2323 3088, ⊛ heritagemalta.org. Daily April–Sept 9am–6pm, Oct–March 9am–5pm. €10.

Fort St. Elmo stands guard at the end of the Sciberras Peninsula on which Valletta is built, erected by the Knights in six months during 1552 in preparation for an imminent invasion by the Turks. Its star shape was intended to provide a defence umbrella of crossfire, and the design undoubtedly worked – St Elmo withstood four weeks of cannon fire from three sides before being captured in the first thrust of the Great Siege of 1565. Later, when Valletta was built, the fort was incorporated within the city's fortifications, and during the seventeenth century the **Carafa Enceinte** was built enclosing the original fort.

Today, the **Rampart** is open to the public for free and is the access point for the recently restored fortress. Malta's marvellous National War Museum, perhaps the best museum in Malta and an essential part of any visit to Valletta, is set within the inner fort.

To access the **National War Museum** – perhaps the best museum in Malta and an essential part of any visit to Valletta – cross the fortress's beautiful inner courtyard before ascending a small staircase to the fort's upper level. Absorbing, interactive exhibits, spread across five halls, take visitors on a journey through Malta's history, which, from the Bronze Age to World War II, was dramatically shaped by military conflict. Highlights include Roosevelt's "Husky" Jeep and "Faith", the sole survivor of the three Gloster Gladiator biplanes that

A Tranquil Star by Anthea Hamilton and Nicholas Byrne, Malta Contemporary Art

performed so bravely in Malta's air defences in 1939. The 1942 George Cross award, given to Malta for its endurance during the intense aerial bombing campaign and blockade that pushed the island to the brink of surrender, is also prominently displayed.

The small but handsome **Chapel of St Anne**, built in 1572 and attributed to Gerolamo Cassar, who also designed the Grand Master's Palace, is worth visiting before your departure. It is roofed by a fine barrel-vaulted ceiling with square coffers and deep mouldings.

The Malta Experience and Sacra Infermeria tour

MAP P.28, POCKET MAP F6
Mediterranean Conference Centre, Hospital St ⊙ 2124 3840, ⊛ mcc.com.mt. July–Oct hourly shows daily 11am–4pm (weekdays) & 11am–2pm (weekends). €16.

The **Malta Experience** is a 45-minute film that tells the story of Malta's seven-thousand-year history, making it a popular first stop for visitors to Valletta. Entry includes a tour of the **Sacra Infermeria** (Holy Infirmary), located across the street, which is best visited after you've picked

St Publius Parish Church

emergency. Its breathtaking main ward – 155m in length with soaring limestone ribbed vaults – was the longest in Europe at the time, and continued to serve as a Station Hospital until after World War I.

Floriana

MAP P.28, POCKET MAP D7

Floriana was created as – and still very much is – a suburb of Valletta, all modest gardens and grids of residential homes. Blink as you enter Valletta by bus and you might miss it, but linger a little longer and you'll notice the village's monuments (look for a golden eagle atop a pillow commemorating RAF victims of World War II) and its massive town square, **Pjazza San Publiju** (Saint Publius Square), so named for its looming church. Frequently the site of open-air concerts and operas during the summer months, Pjazza San Publiju is also commonly referred to as *Il-Fosos* (The Granaries), as it is here that the Knights dug a series of underground chambers to store enough grain to last two years in the event of an invasion and blockade. Today, the stone caps of the now-sealed chambers are still visible across the square.

up some knowledge of Malta's history from the film. While the Knights are famous for repelling an invasion and their various military exploits, they were founded to care for the sick: it is this part of their history that is revealed at the Sacra Infermeria, built in 1574. Once considered amongst the best hospitals in Europe, the Sacra Infermeria could accommodate over nine hundred patients in an

The Floriana Lines

In the 1630s, as the Turks expanded their fleet, the Knights feared a second siege and commissioned Pietro Paolo Floriani (engineer to the pope) to assess Malta's defences. Floriani proposed a line of fortifications across the neck of the Sciberras Peninsula – enclosing Valletta and in effect creating a new fortified suburb, Floriana – so that Malta's entire population could be crammed behind the defences in the event of an invasion. In 1670, the defences were strengthened by means of the Floriana Hornwork, a bulwark jutting out from the Lines' southwest corner, with a fire-range extending across the inner creeks of the Grand Harbour. The Floriana Hornwork and **Portes Des Bombes**, the sole gate through the fortifications, were completed in 1716. The **Floriana Lines** proved the ultimate deterrent: the Turks never attacked, in part because of the virtual impossibility of breaking through the impenetrable fortifications. The handsome Portes Des Bombes is today the primary vehicular entry point to Floriana and Valletta beyond.

Shops

Cek Cik

MAP P.28, POCKET MAP E7
15 Melita St ☎ 7940 2108, ⓦ cekcik.com.
mt. Mon–Fri 10am–6pm, Sat 10am–3pm.
A quirky independent shop with a
unique collection of vintage items,
ceramics, locally designed clothing,
original artwork and beautiful
postcards.

Charles & Ron

MAP P.28, POCKET MAP E6
58D Republic St ☎ 2124 0184,
ⓦ charlesandron.com. Mon–Sat 9am–7pm.
The flagship store of Maltese
haute couture fashion designers
Charles & Ron, where you'll find
their latest collection of wearable
high-end clothing and handbags
with distinctly Maltese imagery and
patterns.

Kir Royal

MAP P.28, POCKET MAP E7
337 St Paul St ☎ 9949 9909, ⓦ kir-royal.
com.mt. Mon & Sun 10am–3pm, Tues–Fri
10am–6.30pm.
Dapper gents will love this
independent boutique with unique
men's apparel, leather goods,
accessories and grooming products.

Marquis de Vissac

MAP P.28, POCKET MAP E7
169 St Lucia St ☎ 7775 5541, ⓦ marquisde
vissac.com. Mon–Sat 10am–6pm.
Dedicated to handmade espadrilles
(unisex, flat wedges) including the
rare French Bayona brand, which
is only stocked in two shops in the
world.

Meli Book Shop

MAP P.28, POCKET MAP E6
185 Old Bakery St ☎ 2123 7266. Mon–Fri
9am–1pm & 4–7pm, Sat 9am–1pm.
A tiny independent bookshop that
looks to have come straight out of
the 1960s, with an excellent stock
of new fiction titles and a vast
selection of books about Malta and
Maltese-language literature.

Mint Sparrow

MAP P.28, POCKET MAP E7
120 St John St ☎ 9995 9519,
ⓦ mintsparrow.com. Mon noon–6pm,
Tues–Fri 10am–6pm, Sat 10am–1pm.
This charming boutique, easily
recognized by its mint green
exterior, offers a curated collection
of hip jewellery, home decor,
artwork and clothing from local
and international designers.

No.Me

MAP P.28, POCKET MAP F6
91B Republic St ☎ 7793 7635,
ⓦ nomestudiovalletta.tumblr.com. Tues–
Sat 10.30am–6pm.
A contemporary Italian design shop
that upcycles discarded items into
clothing, furniture, jewellery and
homeware. The shop's distinctly
styled interior is lovely enough to
be mistaken for an art gallery.

Que

MAP P.28, POCKET MAP E6
50B Old Bakery St ⓦ que.com.mt. Mon
4–7pm, Tues–Fri 10am–noon & 4–7pm, Sat
10am–noon.
A boutique design shop with
wearable art and unique products
created by Maltese artist Enrique
Tabone, whom you can meet at the
shop most days.

Cek Cik

La Mère

Theobroma Cacao Collective

MAP P.28, POCKET MAP E6
123 Old Theatre St ☎ 2124 0304,
Ⓦ theobromacacaocollective.com. Mon–Fri
9am–6.30pm, Sat 10.30am–6pm.
A pretty hole-in-the-wall specializing in (vegan, gluten free and local) desserts and chocolate so delicious you won't notice they're also healthy.

White Shop

MAP P.28, POCKET MAP E7
106E St. John St ☎ 2123 5380,
Ⓦ whiteshopmalta.com. Mon–Fri 10am–
7pm, Sat 10am–5.30pm, Sun 10am–2pm.
A curated selection of handmade women's clothing made from natural silks, linen, bamboo and cashmere with a distinctly relaxed Mediterranean style.

Cafés

Café Jubilee

MAP P.28, POCKET MAP E6
125 St. Lucia St ☎ 2074 2332,
Ⓦ cafejubilee.com. Daily 8am–1am.
There's an intimate atmosphere at long-established vintage-styled

brasserie *Café Jubilee*, so you might just catch bits of gossip from Valletta's politicians, lawyers and police – the national Law Courts are a stone's throw away. Tuck into Nanna's ravioli – you won't find the *dentex* (white fish), lemon and artichoke variety anywhere else – but save room for an authentic Maltese *imqaret* (date-filled pastry) afterwards. Mains €8–13.

Caffe Cordina

MAP P.28, POCKET MAP E6
244 Republic St ☎ 2065 0400,
Ⓦ caffecordina.com. Mon 8am–7pm, Tues,
Fri & Sat 8am–10.30pm, Wed & Thurs
8am–11pm, Sun 8am–3pm.
The 180-year-old, family-run *Caffe Cordina* is a Valletta institution. Service is slow, prices inflated and food mostly average, but it's worth stopping by for a coffee and cake; the tables in front of the National Library are a beautiful spot to watch the world go by, and the interior is richly decorated with paintings by celebrated twentieth-century Maltese painter Giuseppe Cali.

Kingsway

MAP P.28, POCKET MAP E7
57 Republic St ☎ 2099 5757, Ⓦ kingsway
valletta.com. Mon–Sat 8am–11pm.
Of all of the cafés surrounding the National Library, *Kingsway* is a standout, offering a unique vibe that nods to Valletta in its 1930s heyday. With good coffee and fresh croissants (€3), it's an ideal place for a light breakfast, and there's a small menu of well-priced lunch options that changes daily. Free wi-fi.

No. 43

MAP P.28, POCKET MAP E7
43 Merchants St ☎ 2703 2294. Daily
8am–5pm.
Run by an Australian and Italian husband-and-wife team who relocated to Malta from Florence, *No. 43* is one of Malta's best lunch spots, consistently delivering on

its promise of fresh, affordable and healthy food. The menu of anything-but-boring salads (€6) and sandwiches (€5) changes daily. At midday, expect a queue; if you don't manage to get a table, nearby Upper Barrakka gardens (see page 26) makes a great place for a picnic.

Restaurants

Ġuże

MAP P.28, POCKET MAP E6
22 Old Bakery St ☎ 2123 9686, ⓦ guzevalletta.com. Mon–Wed 5.45–10pm, Thurs–Sat 12.30–2.30pm & 5.45–10pm.

Ask any Maltese person for a restaurant recommendation in Valletta and they are likely to say simply: *Ġuże*. And with good reason: located in a charming sixteenth-century building on Old Bakery Street, the well-priced menu here changes seasonally with a focus on local ingredients; expect dishes such as calamari with almonds and lime (€11) and local rabbit with leek and cabbage stuffing (€21). It's best to book in advance as the restaurant's popularity means they can rarely accept walk-ins.

Harbour Club

MAP P.28, POCKET MAP E7
5 Barriera Wharf ☎ 7922 2332, ⓦ theharbourclubmalta.com. Daily 7–11pm.

Located at Barriera Wharf, *Harbour Club*'s breathtaking views and small but superb menu makes it a popular choice among locals for long, leisurely meals. The kitchen offers consistently outstanding local fish and handmade pasta (€12), while the pork served three ways (€24) is a lovely contemporary homage to the Maltese *majjalata* (pig roast) tradition. In the summer, dinner is served outside; in the winter months the dining room is a one-of-a-kind interior: a breathtaking underground cistern. Bookings are necessary on weekends.

is-Suq tal-Belt

MAP P.28, POCKET MAP E7
Merchant St, Valletta ☎ 2210 3500, ⓦ issuqtalbelt.online. Daily 6am until late.

is-Suq tal-Belt (The City Market) was recently restored to its Victorian-era glory, and is the only wrought iron and timber structure in Valletta. A historic site in its own right, visit for the views and stay for the food. Spread over three floors are cafés, an upscale supermarket, and a plethora of food stalls offering everything from fresh pasta and wood fired pizza to Spanish tapas and sushi.

La Mère

MAP P.28, POCKET MAP E7
174 Merchant St ☎ 9949 4721, ⓦ lamere.com.mt. Mon–Sat noon–2.30pm & 7–10.30pm.

La Mère's pan-Asian menu includes everything from curries and tandoori dishes (€15) to vegetable tagine (€16). Particularly recommended are the tasting menu (€38.50) and traditional Indian thali (a platter of rice, curries, salad, naan and sweets for €24.50).

Legligin

MAP P.28, POCKET MAP E6
119 Santa Lucia St ☎ 2122 1699. Daily 1pm–1am.

This charming fifteen-table French-Mediterranean restaurant does not have a menu; patrons pay €25 per head for a multiple-course meal of whatever is fresh and in season (expect soups, wonderful breads and dips, fresh fish and stewed octopus). Wash it all down with one of an array of wines – *legligin* is the Maltese word for the *glug-glug-glug* sound of a generous pour.

Rampila

MAP P.28, POCKET MAP E7
1 St John's Cavalier ☎ 2122 6625, ⓦ rampila.com. Daily 7–10.30pm.

Open for lunch and dinner, *Rampila* is set within Valletta's walls in a romantic vaulted limestone tunnel. The cuisine emphasises rustic Maltese local specialties like rabbit *tortellaci* (stuffed pasta*)* (€13.50) and *bragioli* (thin slices of beef stuffed with egg, beef and minced pork; €19). In the summer, request a table in the pretty garden that overlooks Valletta's City Gate.

Rubino

MAP P.28, POCKET MAP E6
53 Old Bakery St ☏ 2122 4656,
Ⓦ rubinomalta.com. Mon 12.30–2.30pm,
Tues–Sat 12.30–2.30pm & 7.30–10.30pm.
The best place on the island for modestly priced but well-executed local cuisine. The menu is changed every few days, and recurrent seasonal dishes include ox tongue with aubergines and capers (€17), spaghetti with sea urchins (€9) and the dessert *cassata siciliana*, a lovely Italian cheesecake.

Sotto Pizzeria

MAP P.28, POCKET MAP E7
32 South St ☏ 2122 0077. Tues–Sun
12–2.45pm & 6.30–11pm.
Sotto, like its sister restaurant *Zero Sei* (see below), offers hearty Italian cuisine and hospitality. It's an authentic family-run affair specializing in wood-fired pizzas (€12) made with dough that leavens for 72 hours. If pizza isn't for you, the pasta and salads are also good.

Tap Room

MAP P.28, POCKET MAP E6
53 Old Theatre St ☏ 2749 1316,
Ⓦ taproomvalletta.com. Daily 8am–1am.
This hip restaurant offers consistently good food and service. The mussels in cream and champagne (€10) are highly recommended, while the salads, pasta and risottos (€12) are all thoroughly satisfying. Surprisingly, given its name, *Tap Room* doesn't serve many beers, but it does offer an excellent selection of wines (including high-quality labels) by the glass.

Zero Sei

MAP P.28, POCKET MAP E6
75 Old Theatre St ☏ 2122 2010. Daily
noon–2.45pm & 7–11pm.
Located across from the Manoel Theatre, *Zero Sei* is an authentic Roman restaurant where carbonara (including a vegetarian version) is the house speciality. The menu offers excellent value for money with most pastas under €10 and mains under €18. Booking a table here can be difficult; enquire in advance.

Bars

Alchemy

MAP P.28, POCKET MAP E6
93–94 Strait St, Valletta ☏ 9968 9949,
Ⓦ gut.com.mt. Daily 2pm until late.
Alchemy is one of the first bars to re-open in The Gut: the historically most dangerous and sleazy part of Strait Street and its red light district. Keeping its original name and obviously ditching its former vices, Alchemy pushes The Gut upmarket with ultra-modern mixology cocktails and marble-panelled interiors.

Bridge Bar

MAP P.28, POCKET MAP E7
258 St Ursula St ☏ 7947 4227. Daily
8pm–1am.
This place is all about the atmosphere and is especially popular on summer nights, when there can be hundreds jostling for space. If you want a table, book ahead; otherwise join the jovial crowds sitting on the steps. Taking its name from the bridge it is located on, which spans East Street above Victoria Gate, *Bridge Bar* offers live jazz on Fridays under a canopy of bougainvillea and stars (weather permitting).

Café Society

MAP P.28, POCKET MAP E7
13 St John St ☏ 2713 7491, Ⓦ cafesociety
valletta.com. Mon–Sat 5.30pm–1am.

A hip hole-in-the-wall favoured by Malta's artistic set, *Café Society* offers excellent craft beer and cocktails in a quaint, intimate setting. Seating extends onto the steps on St. John's Street: a picturesque setting for watching the moon rise over Birgu's fortifications across the Grand Harbour. In the summer, film screenings are also hosted here.

Charles Grech

MAP P.28, POCKET MAP E7
10 Republic St ☎ 222 8848,
ⓦ charlesgrech.com. Mon–Thurs 8am–11pm, Fri & Sat 8am–1am.
Charles Grech, which can trace its roots back to 1881, is an upmarket and classically styled café bar. Visit after 7pm to snag a table outside for some superb people-watching. Especially appealing at Christmas, when all of Malta makes a pilgrimage to Republic Street for shopping and Valletta's streets glisten with lights.

The Pub

MAP P.28, POCKET MAP F6
136 Archbishop St ☎ 7905 2522. Mon–Thurs & Sun noon–midnight, Fri & Sat noon–1am.
A family-run, English-style pub famed for being the location where British actor Oliver Reed died in 1999 after a heavy drinking session during the making of his last film, *Gladiator*. Occasionally hosts free Shakespeare performances and live music nights.

Trabuxu

MAP P.28, POCKET MAP E7
2 Strait St ☎ 2122 3036, ⓦ trabuxu.com. mt. Tues–Sat 7pm–2am.
A wine bar set in an atmospheric old cellar that attracts a laidback Maltese crowd for its selection of 260 wines – prices start at a modest €15 for a mid-range Maltese Cabernet Sauvignon. Tuck into one of the various platters while jazz and blues music flutters in the background.

Trabuxu

Wild Honey

MAP P.28, POCKET MAP E6
127 St Lucia St ☎ 9990 1859. Mon–Fri noon–1am, Sat 5.30pm–midnight.
An eclectic, relaxed Italian bar serving a variety of craft beers, cocktails and wines. A small but consistently exceptional menu of cheese platters and salads makes this a popular place for couples and groups of friends.

Yard 32

MAP P.28, POCKET MAP E7
32 Strait St ☎ 9993 6734, ⓦ yard32.com. Tues–Sat 6pm–late.
Run by Italians who came to Malta by way of Spain, this tapas and gin bar is one of Malta's best. Knowledgeable staff help patrons select one of two hundred gins and forty tonics, perfectly complemented by a variety of tapas. Live music is offered throughout the week, and a gin-themed aquarium makes this bar lovably quirky.

The Three Cities

Occupying two narrow peninsulas on the other side of the Grand Harbour from Valletta, and enclosed on the land side by Malta's largest defensive fortification, the Three Cities – Birgu, Isla and Borlma – retain a romantic, medieval urban fabric that makes them a pleasure to explore on foot. Atmospheric Birgu has the highest concentration of individual attractions, tucked among winding alleys lined with the residents' informal kerbside gardens. Isla and Borlma both sustained heavy damage during World War II and have no traditional "sights", though a walk along the picturesque promenade from Birgu's marina to Isla offers a lively taste of local life – don't miss the opportunity for a fresh seafood lunch at il-Ħnejja (see page 53). It's also worth strolling just beyond the Three Cities to Kalkara, where Malta's new national science museum, Esplora, is located in a British-era quarantine hospital.

Birgu

MAP P.48, POCKET MAP F8

When the Knights arrived in Malta in 1530, the island's capital city, Mdina, did not suit their naval activities and **Birgu** was elected as the site of their stronghold. The city was hastily fortified and **Fort St Angelo** constructed in anticipation of an impending attack by the Ottoman Empire, which duly arrived in 1565 with the Great Siege, during which the new fortress played a key role (see page 5). After the Great Siege, when reinforcements from Sicily caused the Ottomans to abandon their attack, the Knights began planning a new capital city on Mount Sciberras. When their convent and operations were relocated to Valletta in 1571,

Birgu lost its political importance but continued to operate as a naval base for various occupying forces over the following four centuries. During World War II, several of its key historic attractions were destroyed by bombs, but the city remains endearingly charming.

The best way to explore Birgu is on foot. Enter through the **Three Gates** and get lost in the charming **Collachio**. The **Inquisitor's Palace** and **Maritime Museum** are worth brief interludes. Wander along the city's ramparts and make your way to its harbourfront promenade, which extends from **Fort St Angelo** through the city's new **superyacht marina**. Undoubtedly the most memorable and magical time to visit the city is **Birgufest** (see page 147).

So nice they named them twice

Perhaps owing to their early history (Birgu was the first village settled by the Knights of Malta), the Three Cities are unique in being commonly referred to each by two names: Birgu (Vittoriosa), Isla (Senglea) and Bormla (Cospicua). We use the (more popular) Maltese names in this book.

The Three Gates and Malta At War Museum

MAP P.48, POCKET MAP G9

Until the Three Cities' fortifications were breached for vehicular access, the grandiose, three-tiered **Three Gates** provided the sole entrance to Birgu and they are still the most picturesque way to enter the city. The **Advanced Gate** is the first, designed in 1722 by French architect François de Mondion, also mastermind of the Magisterial Palace in Mdina (see page 66) and Fort Manoel (see page 58). Just beyond the Advanced Gate you will find the **Malta at War Museum** (☎ 2189 6617, ⊕ maltaatwarmuseum.com; daily 10am–4.30pm; €12), which offers an excellent overview of what life was like in Malta during World War II, when the island was more heavily bombed in just one week than London was in the entire Blitz: as many as 100,000 people were displaced within Malta during the war, which destroyed 35,000 homes (the subsequent housing shortage persisted until the 1970s). The museum entrance fee includes an audioguide, free guided tours, a short film screening and access to a fascinating underground air raid shelter: this network of tunnels and small rooms dug into the city's bastion walls includes a surgical ward and birthing room. Within a year and a half, sufficient shelters had been dug into Malta's limestone bedrock to protect the entire island's population.

Opposite the museum is a staircase leading to the **Foss Birgu**, a park in the city's dry moat with mature almond trees and a small meandering path (daily 7am–7/7.30pm). Continuing past the museum takes you over a bridge spanning the moat and through the **Couvre Porte Gate**, the second of the three, which opens into a bare stone courtyard from which centuries' old stairs lead to the ramparts; at the top you get a good

Senglea Marina

view of the complex fortifications. Across this courtyard is the third **Main Gate**; on the other side is Birgu's main village road.

The Collachio

MAP P.48, POCKET MAP G9

Home base of the Knights between 1530 and 1571, the ancient **Collachio** quarter is a perfect place to lose yourself for an hour on a warm afternoon, characterised by pedestrianised, winding alleys that teem with potted plants; the Knights' earliest Baroque townhouses or *auberges* still survive along Triq Hilda Tabone and Triq Il-Majjistral (all have been converted into public buildings or private residences). Historically, the Collachio played witness to the birth of Malta's first Carnival in 1535; the celebrations marking the end of the Great Siege of 1565; and the frequent march of slaves towards Birgu's main square, where regular auctions were once held – slave labour contributed to the building of the Knight's fortifications and persisted in Malta until Napoleon's arrival in 1798. Note the buildings constructed in a 1950s modernist style: they're a sign you're in an area particularly hard hit by World War II air raids.

Visiting the Three Cities

Getting to the Three Cities is straightforward, but it's best to plan ahead: this series of peninsulas look closer than they are, and most routes pass through a series of bays and villages that lengthen your journey. **Buses** #2 & 3 from Valletta passes through Bormla to Birgu, with #3 continuing to Kalkara and Fort Rinella. Bus #4 from Valletta skirts Bormla and terminates at Birgu. A faster and more pleasant way to arrive is by **ferry** from Valletta, departing from Barriera Wharf (descend the lift to the ferry landing from Upper Barrakka Gardens). Ferries depart every 30min (daily June–Oct 6.30am–11.30pm; Nov–May 6.30am–7pm). Fares are €1.50 one-way or €2.80 return (€1.75/3.30 return after 7.30pm). Alternately, you can hire a **traditional wooden boat**, known as a *dghajsa*, to take you across the harbour (specify if you wish to embark at Isla or Birgu when you board). Fares are €2 per person or €12 per boat for transport and a 30min tour of the Grand Harbour. *Dghajsas* queue for passengers next to the ferry. If you plan to return to Valletta by boat, the ferry is a more reliable option; *dghajsas* are independently operated with fluctuating schedules and some require a minimum number of passengers to depart.

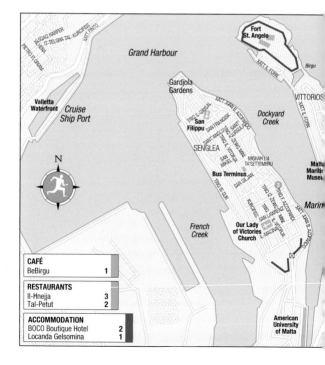

The Inquisitor's Palace

MAP P.48, POCKET MAP G9
Main Gate St, Birgu ☎ 2182 7006,
🌐 heritagemalta.org. Daily 9am–5pm. €6.
Built as law courts in the thirteenth
century, this large Baroque building
became the seat for Malta's
Inquisition between 1574 (when
the Knights departed Birgu) and
1798 (when the French arrived),
and later served as a military
hospital for the British. Your visit
begins on the bottom floor – the
oldest part of the building, virtually
untouched through the ages – with
a short film on the Inquisition,
before continuing through a
compact central courtyard (with
its beautiful ribbed cross-vaults)
to the palace's kitchens. Ascend
a **grand staircase**, designed by
Romano Carapecchia, one of the
most important Baroque artists
working in early medieval Malta,
to the *piano nobile,* the public
domain of the Inquisitor. Here, 3D
models and projections describe
the building's architectural history.
On the top floor you'll encounter
"authentic artefacts confiscated as
proof of misconduct" (primarily
banned books, which were burnt
in front of crowds in Birgu's main
square). Next, descend to the
austere **Tribunal Room**, entered
through a half-sized door intended
to force even the most unwilling of
prisoners to bow to the Inquisitor's
authority. In 1607, Baroque artist
Caravaggio (see page 34) was a
witness in a case of bigamy here.
Round things off with a walk
through the palace's **prisons**, where
the anguished graffiti of internees is
still visible on the walls.

St Lawrence Church

MAP P.48, POCKET MAP G9
St Lawrence St, Birgu.
St Lawrence Church sits
evocatively atop a high parapet
at the town's marina entrance,

THE THREE CITIES

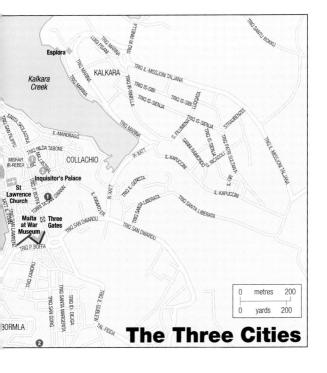

The Three Cities

making it a key part of the village's skyline. The original building was one of Malta's earliest medieval parish churches, and it later served as the Knights' conventual church between 1530 and 1571 until the Knights were transferred to Valletta. The present structure dates from 1681 and was the first of a spate of triumphal churches designed by master Maltese architect Lorenzo Gafa, who shunned the fad for ornate Baroque during his time, achieving a grand presence with architectural setting and composition. The highlight of its interior is the altarpiece by Italian Baroque artist Mattia Preti – a tense depiction of the martyrdom of St Lawrence and Preti's largest ever painting. During World War II, the church suffered multiple bombings, one of which destroyed its dome, later rebuilt in the early 1950s.

Malta Maritime Museum

MAP P.48, POCKET MAP G9
Birgu Waterfront ☎ 2166 0052,
ⓦ heritagemalta.org. Daily 9am–5pm. €5.
Situated in the British-built former naval bakery, the **Maritime Museum** holds an interesting collection pertaining to Malta's illustrious seafaring history. Exhibits consist mainly of models of ships, from the diminutive *dghajsa* to exuberant Knightly galleys. Paintings of famous sea battles, cannons, anchors and salvaged

Malta Maritime Museum

pieces of ships from the past five centuries complete the collection. The largest hall is dedicated to the legacy of the Royal Navy in Malta, from its wartime role to the more recent history of the drydocks at Isla, and includes a charming reconstruction of a sailor's pub.

Fort St Angelo

MAP P.48, POCKET MAP F8
Birgu Waterfront ☎ 2540 1800,
ⓦ heritagemalta.com. Daily April–Sept
9am–6pm; Oct–March 9am–5pm. €8.
Fort St Angelo sits at the tip of Birgu's peninsula, dominating the Grand Harbour with its dramatic vertical layers of limestone fortifications. No other fortress has been as critical in shaping the country's history and, recently restored, it is at long last open to the public.

The history of the fortress dates back to at least the thirteenth century, when the Sicilian overlords kept a small *Castrum Maris* (castle by the sea) here. In 1530, the Knights of the Order of St John took the fort as their headquarters, extensively remodelling it and introducing the bastioned system of defence to Malta. The fort would play a major role in the three-month Great Siege of 1565 as the provisions depot and command centre of Grand Master Jean Parisot de Valette, who led a force of some 600 Knights and a few thousand men-at-arms against over 40,000 Turks – with Fort St Angelo's cannons bombarding the invading forces throughout the Siege, it became a symbol of perseverance and survival against the odds. Over the next three centuries, the fort's defences were continuously strengthened. During World War II, the fortress suffered 69 direct bomb hits owing to its role as the British headquarters, which it relinquished when the Lascaris War Rooms (see page 30) were built. After the war, the fortress remained the shore base of the British navy until 31 March 1979, when the last British sailors left Malta.

Visits begin by climbing ever deeper and higher into the fortress to arrive at the **Ferramolino Cavalier**, located at the fort's southwestern point. Here, three lofty vaults have been transformed into immersive audiovisual experiences (the fort's only formal museum spaces), each describing a different aspect of local history, from the country's millennia of foreign occupation to Fort St Angelo's history and cultural symbolism. After visiting the vaults, you are free to wander about the fortress complex to take in its vast size; climb to the very top for 360-degree views, with the northeastern tip looking out towards Valletta. Access to the Upper Fort is restricted to a limited number of tours and pre-booking is required. Here you'll find **The Magisterial Palace, St Anne's Chapel**, and a private residence for the only resident Knight on the island.

Bormla

MAP P.48, POCKET MAP F9

Bormla (Cospicua), which can trace its origins to megalithic times, has been used by Phoenicians, Romans, Normans and the Knights of St John as a refuge for ships and a hub for commerce and defence. Today, Bormla's motto, *Ingens Amplectitur Agger* (embraced by bastions), perfectly describes the village, which connects the peninsulas of Birgu and Isla (it's often difficult to tell where one village ends and the others begin). A walk along Birgu's pretty harbourfront promenade will bring you to Bormla's Dock 1, which served as the Royal Navy Dockyard and was an important supply base during World War I and World War II. Today, the dockyard is home to the **American University of Malta**.

Bormla's alternate name, *Cospicua*, is a derivative of "conspicuous," so-called because the town lay outside Birgu's fortifications during the Great Siege and was razed to the ground. It was rebuilt and protected by an arc of fortifications (**The Margarita Lines**) that encircle the Three Cities. Eventually, advances in military technology and the modernization of the Ottoman striking armada rendered the Margarita Lines ineffective – an enemy situated on the hillocks outside the wall could lob cannon shells into the Three Cities – and this led to the conception of a second-tier wall beyond the Margarita Lines, called the **Cottonera Lines**. Wholly intact to this day, the Cottonera Lines envelop the Three Cities with a heavy semi-circular wall studded with eight triangular bastions (to facilitate a 360-degree sweep of fire) and two demi-bastions where they connect with the fortifications of Isla and Birgu.

Isla

MAP P.48, POCKET MAP F9

Isla (Senglea) was founded by Knights in the 1550s and takes its name from Claude de la Sengle, Grand Master at the time. Isla was severely damaged in the Great Siege of 1565, and some four hundred years later it was almost completely razed again during World War II. With a population of almost 3000 living in an area of just 0.2 square kilometres, Isla is one of the most densely populated cities in the world, but harbour views on all sides keep it from feeling congested. The best way to access the city is from the promenade opposite Birgu. Climbing any staircase from here will take you to the town's main road, Triq Il-Vitorja, which stretches almost all the way to the tip of the peninsula and offers splendid views of the **marina** to the east (a recently gentrified part of the city) and a **dockyard** to the west (where oil rigs often come in for repairs). The town's parish church, **Our Ladies of Victories**, is in the main square, Misrah Papa Benedittu XV (daily 6–11am & 4–6.45pm; free). It was completely rebuilt after being obliterated during World War II to clear the way for German aircraft to dive-bomb Malta's dockyards.

The highlight of any visit to Isla is the city's oldest area, which survived the war and lies at the tip of Isla's peninsula. The charming alleys and townhouses here are reminiscent of those in Birgu and Valletta yet, located high above and surrounded by the sea on all sides, the neighbourhood offers a distinct flavour. Reaching the end of the peninsula brings you to **Gardjola Gardens** (daily 7am–dusk; free), which is not really a garden but a monument to the *gardjola* (sentry post) that overlooks the harbour here. Take note of the structure's sculpted eye and ear, meant as a warning that the Knights had eyes and ears everywhere. The garden offers excellent views of the Grand Harbour and Fort St Angelo. On Isla's promenade, stop at *il-Ħnejja* (see page 53) for lunch, admiring traditional wooden fishing boats moored next to impressive yachts in the waters separating Isla and Birgu. In late afternoon of summer, local children typically gather here to swim and elderly men to fish.

Fort Rinella

MAP P.48, POCKET MAP H7
Saint Rokku St, Kalkara ☎ 2180 0992, ⦿ fortrinella.com. Daily 9am–5pm. €12, including tour and short film. Bus #3 from Valletta. Free shuttle service (book online).
Particularly for history enthusiasts, **Fort Rinella** is well worth straying off the beaten path for. Lying north of the Three Cities in the town of Kalkara, Fort Rinella was erected by the British in the 1870s specifically to operate the Armstrong 100-ton gun. The largest cannon ever made, it was designed so that its shells could pierce the steel plates of ships as far as three miles away, thereby protecting the sea routes leading to the Grand Harbour. It was fired just forty times, the last in 1905, but it's unclear from historical records whether it ever actually hit anything

it was aimed at. The fort itself is a one of Malta's few examples of Victorian military architecture, and has been sensitively restored by local volunteer group Wirt Artna. Period furnishings and decor have been re-created, and you can study the intricate machinery that operated the Armstrong – the gun is so heavy that it needed a mini coal-fired power station to turn its barrel for aiming. Superb hourly demonstrations and historic re-enactment displays evoke life here during its heyday. The main guided tour (2pm) includes interactive military drills, the firing of period artillery and a cavalry show with charming volunteers and lovingly tended rescue horses.

Esplora

MAP P.48, POCKET MAP G8
Marina St, Kalkara ☎ 2540 1900, ⦿ esplora. org.mt. Tues & Wed 9.30am–4pm, Thurs & Fri 9.30am–9pm, Sat 12.30–9pm, Sun 12.30–7pm. €6 admission, plus €6 for planetarium.
Malta's national interactive science centre, **Esplora**, is located at **Villa Bighi**, built in 1675 as a retirement villa by Fra Giovanni Bichi, an Italian Knight, and occupied for the next century by his descendants and a colourful variety of noblemen. In 1801 the site was identified by Dr J. Stripe, Lord Admiral Nelson's chief physician, as a prime location for a new naval hospital, which fell into disuse after the Royal Navy's departure in 1979. In 2016, Villa Bighi was transformed into Esplora, Malta's newest museum, a splendid, sprawling science centre with plenty besides beautiful views and architecture to occupy the young and young-at-heart. A Planetarium suspended within the ruins of a World War II bombed building is a notable architectural element, but the kitschy films screened here will only appeal to very young visitors. A programme of interactive demonstrations for children changes daily and the on-site café offers standard fare.

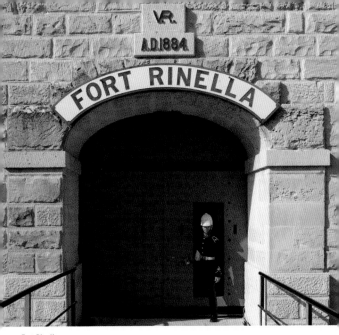

Fort Rinella

Café

BeBirgu

MAP P.48, POCKET MAP G9
Misrah ir-Rebha, Birgu ☎ 7722 0077.
Daily 7am–11pm.

Located in the St Lawrence Band
Club, this relaxed café and bar's
unique, surprisingly palatial
setting makes up for its average
cuisine. Its chefs are Belgian and
German, so mussels and great
German beer are always on the
(affordable) menu.

Restaurants

Il-Ħnejja

MAP P.48, POCKET MAP F9
14 Xatt Juan B Azzopardo, Isla ☎ 7960
3564. Daily 8.30am–3pm & 6.30–11pm.

Eat like a local at il-Ħnejja, an
excellent little family-run place on
Isla's promenade with plenty of
seaside seating. Undoubtedly the
best restaurant in Isla, Il-Ħnejja
offers delicious fresh seafood and

pasta (€10), including lobster
ravioli (€14) and sea urchin
spaghetti (€13). If you can't make
up your mind on what to order,
the restaurant will serve a platter
of various pastas.

Tal-Petut

MAP P.48, POCKET MAP G9
20 Pacifiku Scicluna St, Birgu ☎ 2189 1169
or 7942 1169, ⊛ talpetut.com. Mon–Sat
6.30–10pm, Sun by reservation.

Unmissable *Tal-Petut* offers a
"private dining" experience which,
owing to the warm hospitality of
cook and host, Donald Caligari
Conti (who never forgets a
name or face), manages to be
intimate, elegant and relaxed at
once. There's no menu here, just
a multi-course experience (€28)
of the best Maltese food that
takes "made from scratch" to new
heights (Donald even sun-dries
the tomatoes), employing fresh,
seasonal ingredients according to
the restaurant's motto: "Mother
Nature is the chef; we are
the cooks."

Sliema and St Julian's

Malta's cosmopolitan hub sprawls along its rocky coastline for some 5km, from the harbourfront villages of Gżira and Sliema to the nightlife hubs of St Julian's and Paceville. These two relatively young towns emerged as the island's entertainment centres in the 1980s; in the 1990s a string of luxury hotels and condominiums pushed the area further upscale. Modern facilities pull in the tourists, and despite having no historic attractions, good transport connections make the area a convenient base, while remaining close to the nightlife scene.

Sliema and St Julian's

MAP P.56, POCKET MAP A2–E5

Once quiet fishing hamlets, Sliema and St Julian's became urban hubs in the nineteenth century when Valletta residents built colourful Victorian summer homes and the British installed coastal fortifications here. Sadly, both are disappearing to make way for modern skyscrapers, but this juxtaposition of old and new is part of this area's unique character.

Promenade in Sliema

Sliema and St Julian's are synonymous with the sea and shopping. A stroll along the pretty seaside **promenade** they share is an essential part of any visit. Begin at Gżira's Manoel Island (see page 55) and you can follow the coastline for 5km to St Julian's Spinola Bay. The stretch that faces Valletta's skyline is The Strand, Malta's main shopping district. This leads to Tigne Point, a luxury residential complex and shopping mall. Tigne Point connects on to Tower Road, the main stretch of the promenade facing a wide rocky shoreline beloved by tourists, teenage English-language students and local families for swimming and seaside BBQs. During the summer, the majority of this shoreline is a protected swimming zone (if you prefer a dip in a pool, visit a nearby lido; see page 58). In the winter, rough seas make swimming here inadvisable, but sea views from the promenade are still captivating (and the star attraction of a staggering number of restaurants and bars).

There are a few historic points of interest too. During the 1565 Great Siege, Ottoman Admiral Dragut Rais stationed his troops at Sliema's Tigne Point, where he was killed in a bombardment. In 1789, St Julian's entered the

Traditional colourful Maltese balconies in Sliema

history books as the first town to be conquered in the French occupation (Spinola Bay is believed to be where Napoleon landed).

Gżira

MAP P.56, POCKET MAP B5

Gżira, Sliema's less glamorous, less expensive sister village, is the starting point for the promenade (see page 54) that extends to St Julian's. The village enjoys lovely views of Valletta's skyline, although a busy marina means there are no swimming zones here. Gżira is named after nearby **Manoel Island** (*gżira* means "island"), where visitors can cross a short bridge to

Visiting Sliema and St Julian's

Sliema and St Julian's are well served by **buses** (publictransport.com.mt), with frequent stops along the promenade (see page 54) and a few routes through the villages' centres. The main bus terminal is located in Sliema, where a ferry connects Sliema to Valletta at the aptly named Sliema Ferries area. Hop-on hop-off tour buses also stop throughout Sliema and St Julian's, some calling at specific hotels and resorts. Sliema and St Julian's have Malta's highest concentration of **Next Bikes** (rental bicycles; see page 139).

It's difficult to find a **parking spot** in Sliema and St Julian's congested streets. Your best bet is the multi-storey car park on High Street in Sliema's shopping zone; in St Julian's try Spinola Park (Mikiel Ang Borg Street, Spinola Bay), Eden Park (St Augustine Street, Paċeville) or the more expensive car park at Portomaso (Portomaso Road; €10/24hr). For **taxis**, try St Julian's-headquartered eCabs (☎ 2138 3838, 🖥 ecabs.com.mt), Yellow Cabs (☎ 2298 2298, 🖥 yellowcabsmalta.com) or Greenr (☎ 2738 3838, 🖥 greenr.cab), all of which operate 24/7.

Sliema and St Julian's

ACCOMMODATION	
115 The Strand Suites	19
Boho Hostel	17
Cavalieri Art Hotel	11
Corinthia Hotel St George's Bay	1
The District Hotel	6
The George	5
Hilton	8
Hostel Malti	13
Hostel Med	10
Hotel Juliani	12
Hotel Valentina	7
Inhawi Boutique Hostel	14
InterContinental Malta	3
Onyx Suites & Apartments	9
The Palace	16
Pebbles Boutique Aparthotel	18
PV Hostel	4
The Victoria	15
Westin	2

SHOPS	
Christine X Art Gallery	3
Fly the Fly Vintage	4
Soap Café	1
Souvenirs That Don't Suck	2

RESTAURANTS	
Ali Baba	14
Café Cuba	2
Electro Lobster Project	10
Kebab Ji	9
New York Best	1, 12
Piccolo Padre	6
U Bistrot	8
Zest	3

CAFÉS	
Fre{n}sch	11
il-Gabbana	4
Marks & Spencer Café	13
Maxim Jr's The Maltese Tea Room	7
Mint	5

BARS AND CLUBS	
Black Gold	8
Club Havana	2
Hammett's Gastro Bar	7
Hole in the Wall	6
Hugo's Terrace	1
The Scotsman Pub	5
The Thirsty Barber	3
Twenty Two	4

Lidos

If you prefer pools to the sea, visit one of Sliema or St Julian's many freshwater **lidos**, typically open from 9am–7pm. Popular establishments include Neptune's (€6–8, Spinola Bay; ⓦ neptuneswpsc.com), Pearl Beach (€15, Sliema; ⓦ pearlbeachmalta.com) and MedAsia Playa (€10–15, Sliema; ⓦ medasia.com.mt/playa). Many hotels and resorts in Sliema and St Julian's also offer day memberships to their pools, including the Corinthia Hotel St George's Bay (€20–25; see page 130), the Radisson Blu (€20–30; ⓦ radissonblu.com), the Hilton (€25–38; see page 131) – a great option for travellers staying at B&Bs or apartments.

find a duck sanctuary and, in the summer months, a small outdoor fair. The island is dominated by **Fort Manoel**, a beautiful eighteenth-century fortification enclosing a magnificent parade ground and arcade, which is not currently open to visitors – public pressure may see this change in the coming years.

Balluta Bay
MAP P.56, POCKET MAP B3

Sliema slides imperceptibly into St Julian's at **Balluta Bay**, with its busy seaside promenade and

small triangular *pjazza*. Peppered with Judas trees, benches and a few cafés, the square is a nice place for an afternoon drink. Its eastern flank is dominated by the monumental Balluta Buildings, a fantastic 1920s Art Nouveau apartment block whose arches, intricate angel motifs and terraced profile provide an ornate contrast to the otherwise uniform high-rises fringing the bay. Though shallow and sometimes silty, the bay itself is a swimming zone and home to the lido Neptune's (see above).

Balluta Bay

Spinola Bay

Spinola Bay

MAP P.56, POCKET MAP A2–B2

Home to legions of restaurants, cafés, bars and hotels, compact, kidney-shaped **Spinola Bay** is always bustling with people strolling along the promenade and watching the fishermen mending nets in front of their boathouses. The bay itself remains home to a dwindling number of moored-up *luzzu*, painted in vibrant colours, decorated with Baroque designs and sporting the much-photographed "Eyes of Osiris" on their bows to lead to good fishing grounds. Many of Spinola Bay's restaurants have terraces overlooking the sea, making it a lovely spot to have dinner, with the lights shimmering romantically and the *LOVE* monument (designed by Richard England in 2003) reflecting in the bay's still water.

Paċeville

MAP P.56, POCKET MAP B2

Paċeville is Malta's prime nightlife district, with dozens of bars, clubs, pubs and "gentlemen's clubs" rubbing shoulders at ground level, and high-rise resort-style apartment blocks towering overhead. Deserted by day, Paċeville picks up at night, when thousands of young people descend on the quarter (peak hours are between 11pm and 3am). It's a boisterous, cheap, cheerful and generally amicable scene, with loud music blaring from the open-fronted bars and people spilling onto the pavements. You'll find a more mature crowd at the bars in Sliema or Valletta. If clubbing isn't your scene, Paċeville also offers a small sandy beach (St George's Bay), the Bay Street shopping mall, the seventeen-screen Eden Cinemas and the Eden Bowling Alley.

Shops

Christine X Art Gallery

MAP P.56, POCKET MAP D4

17 Triq Tigne, Sliema ☏ 9984 4652,
Ⓦ christinexart.com. Mon–Sat 10am–1pm
& 4–7pm.

A small but excellent art gallery
exclusively stocking local works,
from Maltese landscapes to
figurative pieces.

Fly the Fly Vintage

MAP P.56, POCKET MAP D4

6 Triq Manwel Dimech, Sliema ☏ 9938
2377, Ⓦ flythefly.com. Mon–Fri 10am–7pm,
Sat 11am–6pm.

This quirky shop, run by a Swedish
team, offers elegant, one-of-a-kind
vintage clothing and accessories
from the 1950s to 1990s for men
and women.

Soap Café

MAP P.56, POCKET MAP C4

46 Triq Santa Marija, Sliema ☏ 2788
3675, Ⓦ soapcafemalta.com. Mon–Fri
4.30p–7.30pm, Sat 10.30am–2pm.

As its name suggests, *Soap Café* is a
boutique specializing in handmade
soaps, lotions, balms and scrubs
made from local ingredients like
olive oil, goat's milk and purees of
local prickly pears and pumpkins.
Airline-friendly sizes of most
products are available.

Souvenirs That Don't Suck

MAP P.56, POCKET MAP C4

108 Triq Manwel Dimech, Sliema ☏ 7907
2313, Ⓦ souvenirsthatdontsuck.com. Mon–
Fri 10am–7pm, Sat 11am–6pm.

That rare thing: a hip souvenir
shop. Look for hoodies with the
ubiquitous local phrase, "Mela",
a word completely unique to the
Maltese language, used to mean
anything from "so" or "yes" to an
expression of surprise.

Cafés

Fre{n}sch

MAP P.56, POCKET MAP B3

37 Triq Ġorġ Borg Olivier, St Julian's
☏ 2137 0818, Ⓦ frenschbakes.com. Tues–

Christine X Art Gallery

Sun 7.30am–6pm.

A small French patisserie and boulangerie where everything is made by hand. Try the *millefeuille* with fresh *crème pâtissière* (€3).

il-Gabbana

MAP P.56, POCKET MAP D3

Triq it-Torri, Sliema ☏ 2701 1527, Ⓦ ilgabbana.com. Daily 9am–midnight.

Essentially an upscale kiosk, *il-Gabbana* offers lovely sea views and a large outdoor terrace. Salads, pasta, pizza and burgers (€10–15) are average but for a perfect light bite, the *focaccia semplice* is highly recommended.

Marks & Spencer Café

MAP P.56, POCKET MAP D4

Triq it-Torri, Sliema ☏ 2133 1745. Mon–Thurs 11am–3pm & 5.30–10pm, Fri 11am–2pm & 5.30–11pm, Sat 5–11pm, Sun 5–10pm.

Before you write it off as a boring chain, consider this: Mark's & Spencer's Sliema café boasts quite possibly the best view of the Valletta skyline. The food is surprisingly good, too, and the prices reasonable.

Maxim Jr's The Maltese Tea Room

MAP P.56, POCKET MAP B3

256 Triq it-Torri, St Julian's ☏ 9944 7767. Daily 7am–10pm.

This casual Italian-run café specializes in local and Italian treats, including *pastizzi, arancini* (fried, cheese-stuffed rice balls) and an excellent selection of traditional Italian sweets and cakes.

Mint

MAP P.56, POCKET MAP D3

30 Triq Windsor, Sliema ☏ 2133 7177, Ⓦ mintmalta.com. Wed–Sun 8am–4pm.

Established by a few creative Kiwis as a typical New Zealand-style café, *Mint* is now very popular amongst Malta's expats, offering fresh, organic and home-made lunch options – salads, sandwiches, savoury bakes and sweet treats –

at reasonable prices (dine in or takeaway).

Restaurants

Ali Baba

MAP P.56, POCKET MAP B5

9 Triq Ponsomby, Gżira ☏ 2134 0119, Ⓦ hanyharb.com. Mon 6.30–10.30pm, Tues–Fri noon–3pm & 6.30–10.30pm, Sat 6.30–10.30pm.

Malta's first Lebanese restaurant was opened over 25 years ago and they still make everything by hand, from the pitta bread to each and every mouthwatering mezze – ordering a selection to share is highly recommended (€4–17 each).

Café Cuba

MAP P.56, POCKET MAP A2

159 Triq San Ġorġ, Spinola Bay, St Julian's ☏ 2010 2323, Ⓦ cafecuba.com.mt. Daily 8am–11pm.

Its name suggests otherwise, but *Café Cuba*'s focus is Mediterranean food, including excellent wood-fired pizzas (€8–12) and focaccia made with ingredients imported from Italy. Of its two locations in Sliema and St Julian's, the latter offers the loveliest atmosphere, with a large terrace overlooking pretty Spinola Bay.

Electro Lobster Project

MAP P.56, POCKET MAP B3

32 Triq Ġorġ Borg Olivier, Balluta Bay, St Julian's ☏ 2735 7357, Ⓦ electrolobsterproject.com. Daily: restaurant 5–11pm; bar 5pm till late.

Located in the beautiful 1920s Balluta Buildings, the house speciality at this restaurant (upper levels) and trendy lounge (lower level; DJ or live music at weekends) is, unsurprisingly, lobster and fresh seafood, which finds its way into salads, pastas and even burgers.

Kebab Ji

MAP P.56, POCKET MAP D3

124 Triq it-Torri, Sliema. Daily 11am–2am.

Piccolo Padre

This casual Lebanese offers reliably good and affordable salads, kebabs, falafel, pita and *shawarma* prepared fresh to order (mixed plates, €10). Busy at all hours with takeaway custom, there are also a few tables for eating in.

New York Best

MAP P.56, POCKET MAP D4
Sliema Seafront, Qui-Si-Sana and Triq Paceville, St Julian's ☎ 2728 2899, Ⓦ newyorkbest.com. Daily 9am–11pm.
This hip local burger chain, with locations in Sliema and St Julian's, was the first in Malta to offer indulgent upscale fast food (burgers, hot dogs, pizzas, milkshakes) made with an emphasis on local ingredients. Dine in or takeaway.

Piccolo Padre

MAP P.56, POCKET MAP B3
195 Triq Ġorġ Borg Olivier, St Julian's ☎ 2134 4875, Ⓦ piccolopadre.com. Mon–Sat 6.15–11pm, Sun noon–3pm & 6.15–11pm.
Expect some of the best pizzas in Malta at this rustic Italian *trattoria*, which sits right on top of the sea in Balluta Bay. Try the *pizzotto l'originale* with sesame seeds,

mozzarella, mushrooms, gorgonzola and local honey (€10). Also offers pasta (€10–12), local rabbit (€17) and veggie options.

U Bistrot

MAP P.56, POCKET MAP B3
195 Triq Ġorġ Borg Olivier, St Julian's ☎ 2134 4875. Mon–Fri 10am–11pm, Sat & Sun 9am–midnight.
A popular bistro overlooking Balluta Bay serving a small but excellent healthy, seasonal menu (including low-calorie options). Before noon, try the reliable full English and delicious pancakes and eggs Benedict. For lunch and dinner, expect salads, pastas, homemade burgers and grilled fish.

Zest

MAP P.56, POCKET MAP A2
25 Triq San Ġorġ, St Julian's ☎ 2138 7600, Ⓦ zestflavours.com. Mon–Sat 7–11pm.
Zest introduced the Asian Fusion concept to Malta in 2002 and has been a favourite amongst locals since. House specialities include Indonesian beef rendang (€25) and top notch sushi (€8–13). During the summer, tables on the restaurant's small terrace offer lovely sunset views.

Bars and clubs

Black Gold

MAP P.56, POCKET MAP C5
Triq Ix-Xatt, Gżira ☎ 2133 4808. Daily 7am–4am.
This casual watering hole is more of a café-style joint during the day. In the evenings it morphs into a more boisterous and beer-fuelled bar, especially on weekends when it's likely to stay open until early morning. The music is a mix of rock and other genres, and sports matches are regularly shown.

Club Havana

MAP P.56, POCKET MAP A1
86 Triq San Ġorġ, Paċeville ☎ 2137 4500. Daily 10pm–4am.

Despite its reputation as a pick-up joint, this club remains popular and is usually full (and sweaty) at weekends with a young crowd. The ground floor specializes in hip-hop, while the upper level leans more towards r'n'b and soul.

Hammett's Gastro Bar

MAP P.56, POCKET MAP D4
33/34 Tigne Seafront, Sliema ☎ 2134 1116, ⊕ hammettsgastrobar.com. Daily 11am–1am.

This gastro bar, located in Sliema's busy shopping district, is at its busiest for aperitivo, when stylish shoppers take residence to catch up on gossip over cocktails and tapas.

Hole in the Wall

MAP P.56, POCKET MAP D4
31 Triq Kbira, Sliema ☎ 9980 8386, ⊕ holeinthewall.com.mt. Mon–Fri 8.30am–1am, Sat & Sun 5pm–1am.

Tucked on a quiet side street just off of Sliema's main shopping area, this ninety-year-old pub has some of the most affordable prices in this (typically overpriced) village. Despite its diminutive size, it frequently hosts top-notch gigs with Malta's best and up-and-coming acts.

Hugo's Terrace

MAP P.56, POCKET MAP A1
St. George's Bay, Paceville ☎ 2137 6767, ⊕ hugosterrace.com. Daily noon–4am.

A comfortable lounge popular with a more mature crowd of locals and expats that offers a dance floor (with DJs mixing lounge and house music) within sight of St. George's Bay Beach.

The Scotsman Pub

MAP P.56, POCKET MAP A2
62 Triq San Ġorġ, Paceville ☎ 2135 3660. Mon–Sat 11am–late & Sun 11.30am–late.

Think fish and chips, full English breakfasts, roast Sunday dinners (€9.95) and a generally British clientele. Also authentically British is the drunkenness on show at the pub's karaoke nights (Thurs–Sun).

Major sports matches regularly screened.

The Thirsty Barber

MAP P.56, POCKET MAP A1
Triq Ball, St Julian's ☎ 7944 0909, ⊕ the thirstybarber.com. Mon–Thurs 6pm–late, Fri & Sat 5pm–late, Sun 3pm–midnight.

A hip, speakeasy-themed cocktail bar with a "hidden" entrance through a red telephone box. The upmarket menu revives typical Prohibition recipes, such as the Paper Plane (created in London's Ritz Hotel in the 1920s), prepared with Brazilian lime juice and Amaro Nonino.

Twenty Two

MAP P.56, POCKET MAP B2
Level 22, Portomaso Business Tower, St Julian's ☎ 7969 9222, ⊕ 22.com.mt. Wed–Sun 9.30–4am.

Twenty Two is all about superlatives: it's the country's poshest, most exclusive club (with prices to match), with the best views from atop Malta's tallest building. Expect a mature, affluent, smartly dressed crowd enjoying chill-out tunes. There's usually a nominal cover charge and reservations are essential on weekends.

Hole in the Wall

Mdina and Rabat

With everything from Malta's ancient capital, frozen in time, to rolling green valleys and the rugged heights of the nearby coast, the island's western region has a distinct feel and allure, and should be a part of any itinerary. Start with Mdina, a majestic pedestrianized village enclosed by early medieval fortifications, before hitting its neighbour, Rabat, which has an eclectic mix of underground sights from the same period. To the west lie Malta's largest woodland and the dramatic Dingli Cliffs, which tumble down to Fomm Ir-Riħ, a wildly beautiful bay.

Mdina

MAP P.66, POCKET MAP D14

With views of most of the country from atop its golden ring of fortifications, tiny, achingly beautiful **Mdina** is one of Malta's major highlights. One of the island's earliest urban settlements, it also served as the capital until Valletta took over in 1571. First established by the Phoenicians and later taken over by the Romans (who named it Melite),

Old street, Mdina

ancient Mdina used to be up to three times its current size. Legend has it that when Paul the Apostle was shipwrecked in Malta in 60 CE, he was greeted by Publius, the governor of Melite, who became the first Bishop of Malta. Few remains survive from the Roman period, with the most significant at Domus Romana (see page 69). As the Western Roman Empire fell and Melite slid into the early medieval era, a dry moat was built, reducing the city to its present size.

The village's mazes of narrow, twisting alleys were designed to disorient invading forces and today maintain their distinctly medieval feel. With tumbling pink bougainvillea and pretty archways, photo opportunities here abound. The Knights could not resist adding a Baroque flair to the city in the eighteenth century with the addition of the Main Gate and Magisterial Palace (see page 66), both picturesque in their own right. Virtually car-free and with just three hundred inhabitants (including cloistered nuns and several noble families), by night Mdina feels frozen in time under a cloak of silence. By day, it's a regular haunt for tour groups but, nonetheless, an unforgettable setting.

A Mdina walking tour

If you only have an hour or so here, forget street names and let your feet and eyes guide you through Mdina's series of small *pjazzas* and winding alleys (the village is so small it's impossible to remain lost for long). Don't overlook the lovely coats of arms and elaborate bronze door-knockers adorning many facades.

If you prefer a more focused walking tour, follow Mdina's main street – Triq Villegaignon – which connects Mdina end-to-end. The village's most exuberant palaces and several cloisters find their address here, and the street also leads to the main square, Pjazza San Pawl, where you can't miss the huge Cathedral of St Paul. Further on is Palazzo Santo Sofia, one of Mdina's oldest buildings, recognisable from the street-tunnel that cuts through its ground floor, and a fine example of Siculo-Norman architecture (a hybrid of Norman and Sicilian styles found only in Malta). At the end of Triq Villegaignon, Bastion Square is backed by elegant houses and dotted with ficus trees; from here – 140m above sea level – you can admire the expansive view of nearly half the country from one of Malta's highest points. To the southeast, the skyline of Valletta and St Julian's are easily discernible and, to northeast, the Mosta Dome (see page 75).

The Main Gate and Pjazza San Publiju

MAP P.66

Mdina's Main Gate was a Baroque contribution by the Knights built in 1724. It formed part of a restoration programme overseen by Grand Master Manoel de Vilhena, which saw the gate shifted east (you can still see the outline of its medieval predecessor to one side) so that it would lead

Mdina's Main Gate

Inside St Paul's Cathedral

directly to the planned Magisterial Palace. Below the gate is a dry moat, recently turned into a pretty public garden that is accessible by descending the stairs below *Il-Veduta* restaurant to the southeast. Mind your step as you enter the Main Gate, which is frequented by horse-drawn carriages called *karrozin* – a rather unnecessary tourist trap in this perfectly compact, pedestrianized town.

Magisterial Palace

MAP P.66
Pjazza Publiju.

Built in 1724, the Magisterial Palace was designed by French architect François de Mondion under the patronage of Grand Master de Vilhena, who spent his summers here away from public life in Valletta. The palace's interior was first pared down when it was converted into a hospital under British rule, and

Mdina and Rabat

TRIQ L-IMTARFA
TRIQ IL-MALTIN INTERNATI U EŻILJATI
TRIQ GĦERIEXEM
TRIQ DG
TRIQ DONI L-QADIMA
TRIQ IL-Q INDRI BI
TRIQ BIR IL-LJUN
TRIQ GĦERIEXEM
TRIQ SANTA RITA
TRIQ TONI FARRUĠIA
TRIQ PAWLU INGUANEZ
TRIQ IR-RUMANI
TRIQ SANTA BARBARA
TRIQ SANTA RITA
TRIQ IR-REBĦA
TRIQ GĦAJN KAJJET
TRIQ BIR IR-RIEBU
TRIQ PIERRE MUSCAT
TRIQ BIR IR-RIEBU
TRIQ SANTA RITA
TRIQ BIR IR-RIEBU
VJAL IL-ĦADDIEM
TRIQ EMMANUEL VITALE
MISR IL-PARĊ
Wignacourt Museum
TRIQ MONS. A. BUHAĠIAR
TRIQ IL-ĦEMS
TRIQ IN-NIGRET
TRIQ IL-ĦABEL IZA
St Paul's Catacombs
RABAT
TRIQ SANTA SCATTIA
TRIQ IL-FEJGEL
St Agatha's Catacombs and Museum

| 0 | metres | 200 |
| 0 | yards | 200 |

Visiting Mdina and Rabat

Mdina and Rabat are reached on **buses** #51, #52, #53 and #56 from Valletta, #65 from Sliema and #86 from Buġibba. Bus #81 from Valletta passes Mdina and Rabat and continues to Il-Buskett and Dingli Cliffs. There are two public **car parks** between Mdina and Rabat, and both villages are easily (and best) explored on foot.

further ruined in 1973 when it was reopened as the Museum of Natural History (☎ 2145 5951, ⓦ heritagemalta.org; daily 9am–5pm), with a worn-out collection that is hardly worth perusing. Do take a look at the palace's elegant facade, though, which survives intact.

St. Paul's Cathedral

MAP P.66
Pjazza San Pawl ⓦ metropolitanchapter. com. Mon–Sat 9.30am–5pm; Sun 3–5pm; Mass at 9am and 6pm (free). €5 for the Cathedral and museum.

The seat of the Archdiocese of Malta (a function shared with St John's Co-Cathedral; see page 33), **St Paul's Cathedral** majestically dominates the skyline for miles around. Dedicated to Malta's most venerated saint, it was built to replace an earlier twelfth-century cathedral that collapsed in a major earthquake that collapsed in 1693 (the 7.4 magnitude quake also devastated Sicily and badly damaged buildings in Valletta and the Three Cities). It was designed by the best-known Maltese architect of the time, Lorenzo Gafa, who, unlike his

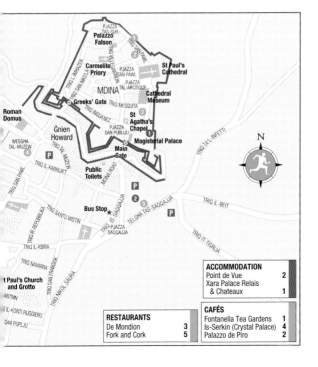

peers, shunned the ornateness of Baroque. Gafa achieved a grand presence by designing a facade with square proportions, the width equal to the height, a stylistic technique that is unusual in churches. The two clocks on the facade are a nineteenth-century addition; one shows the hour, the other the calendar.

Mdina's cathedral offers a more restrained interior compared to St John's Co-Cathedral's celebration of knightly excess. At ground level, six modest side chapels contribute to a sombre atmosphere, and 134 variegated marble tombstones patchwork the floor of the nave, marking the graves of venerated clerics and laymen from noble families. Two large and atmospheric paintings by Mattia Preti in the chancel survive from the original Norman church. Crane your neck higher and you are rewarded with an abundance of ceiling frescoes and gold gilding, beautifully lit by the windows lining the cathedral's uppermost level. The ceiling frescoes depict

Palazzo Falson

the life of St Paul, painted by Sicilian brothers and artists Vincenzo, Antonio and Francesco Manno in the eighteenth century; the frescoes inside the dome are the nineteenth-century work of Giuseppe Gallucci.

Cathedral Museum

MAP P.66
Pjazza tal-Arcisqof ☎ 2145 4697,
ⓦ metropolitanchapter.com. Same ticket and hours as cathedral.
Across the road from the cathedral (and included in your ticket), the **Cathedral Museum** is a repository for the cathedral's moveable arts accumulated over the centuries. Housed in the former Diocesan Seminary, a Baroque palace built 1733–40, it is the largest private museum in Malta. An entire room is dedicated to the museum's excellent collection of German Renaissance artist Albrecht Dürer's woodcuts and copper plates, donated to the museum in 1831 by French Count Saverio Marchese (1757–1833). Additional exhibitions of note include an extensive silver and coin collection, ecclesiastical vestments, original manuscripts, ancient reliquaries, an Annunciation altarpiece by French artist Antoine de Favray, and – perhaps the most impressive piece in the museum – a huge fifteenth-century polyptych by Luis Borrassa showing scenes from the life of St Paul.

Palazzo Falson

MAP P.66
Triq il-Villegaignon ☎ 2145 4512,
ⓦ palazzofalson.com. Tues–Sun 10am–5pm. €10.
Palazzo Falson is the best surviving example of the style of two-storey Siculo-Norman medieval palace favoured by Sicilian, Spanish and local nobility in Mdina. This fascinating private museum's collection of historical art includes paintings, silver items,

Kitchen in the Carmelite Priory

furniture, jewellery and "Oriental" rugs. A compact and beautiful library contains over 4500 books and valuable manuscripts, while on the walls of the Armoury an array of swords, pole arms, pistols and guns are on display. The collection was amassed by Olof Gollcher, who bought the house in 1927 and spent his vast wealth (inherited from his family's shipping line) on filling it with treasures scavenged during his travels. Highlights of the collection include a Robert Robin fob watch with a ten-hour dial that still tells French Revolutionary time (perhaps one of the few that still exist) and several good paintings, including Mattia Preti's *Lucretia Stabbing Herself*, and Edward Lear's take on the idyllic and tranquil coastal landscapes in Malta. An audioguide included with the entry ticket helps explain the displays.

Carmelite Priory

MAP P.66
Triq il-Villegaignon ☎ 2145 4524,
ⓦ carmelitepriory.org. Open by appointment.

The seventeenth-century Carmelite Priory in Mdina is the only priory in Malta open to visitors. The highlight of any visit is the Refectory (where friars congregated for communal meals) – no surface is left untouched by pastel frescoes, pink damask, trompe l'oeil paintings and marble. Other rooms provide a glimpse of friars' daily life. Tours end at the adjoining Carmelite Church, with its spectacular egg-shaped dome and candy-floss pink interior.

Roman Domus

MAP P.66
Wesgħa tal-Mużew, Mdina ☎ 2145 4125,
ⓦ heritagemalta.org. Daily 9am–5pm. €6.
A repository for most of Malta's small collection of Roman relics, the **Roman Domus** museum is built around the remains of its star attraction, a Roman villa that was unearthed in 1881. It dates from around 50 CE, and is one of twenty-five Roman villas in Malta that are thought to have served as the homesteads of large agricultural estates, probably producing olive oil. The location

Feast of St Joseph

of this building on the outskirts of Mdina (then Malta's de facto capital), as well as the life-sized statues discovered within of Emperor Claudius and his mother Antonia, suggest that it belonged to a senior Roman figure. Now only the peristyle, with a splendid mosaic floor depicting the drinking doves of Sosos (a famous and popular motif of antiquity, which can also be seen in Pompeii and Rome), survives from the original house. Tours end at the adjoining Muslim cemetery, established in the eleventh century and home to at least 245 burial sites. Artefacts discovered during excavations here are also on display inside the Roman villa, including limestone sarcophagi and tombstones inscribed with beautiful, looping Kufic script.

Rabat

MAP P.66, POCKET MAP D14–15

Five minutes' walk south of Mdina along charming Triq San Pawl brings you to Rabat's town square, to which Mdina's walls stretched until Arab rule (870–1090 CE). The Arabs rebuilt the fortifications on a smaller scale for better defensibility, in effect creating a new suburb (rabat means suburb in Arabic), which eventually grew into a town. The most charming part of Rabat are a series of winding narrow streets (mostly devoid of cars) on the boundary between Mdina and Rabat, well worth exploring by foot. On March 19th the village's celebrates its largest *festa* (dedicated to St Joseph, also a public holiday), during which this area is beautifully decorated in enormous pale blue, white and gold banners and twinkling lights.

St Paul's Catacombs

MAP P.66

Triq Sant Agata, Rabat ☎ 2145 4562, ⓦ heritagemalta.org. Daily 9am–5pm. €5.
Rabat's main sight, **St Paul's Catacombs**, date back to the time when Rabat was part of Mdina and early Christians buried their dead outside the city walls. This dark maze of burial chambers, dug in the fourth and fifth centuries, offers the earliest archaeological evidence of Christianity in Malta. Although small compared to Rome's catacombs, the site offers a good

example of Maltese underground architecture, a wholly unique development that was barely influenced by outside traditions.

A visit begins at the excellent visitor centre, which offers a brief introduction to burial traditions and artefacts as well as a short film. Cross the street to enter the underground complex, which first presents two large halls. An interesting feature of the catacombs found here is the Agape table, likely used in funerary rituals where a final meal was shared between living and deceased. From here, raised pathways and atmospheric lighting propel you forward through the labyrinthine passageways. A number of different terraced levels cover an area of over two thousand square metres, and more than a thousand sarcophagi occupying every conceivable space.

St Paul's Church, Wignacourt Museum and Grotto

MAP P.66
Triq ir-Rebha, Rabat ⓣ 2749 4905,
ⓦ wignacourtmuseum.com. Daily 9.30am–5pm. €5 for the three sites; audioguide €2.

St Paul's Catacombs

Rabat's town square is dominated by **St Paul's Church**, which stands on a site where a church is known to have existed since 1372 (though the present Baroque building dates from 1653). Designed by Francesco Buonamici (who introduced Baroque architecture to Malta) it has an unusually wide, squat facade. For a church with such a lengthy history, the interior is surprisingly bare and bland. The adjoining Wignacourt Museum presents a series of liturgical artefacts and religious paintings.

St Paul's **grotto** is said to have been the hiding place of the saint during his three-month stint in Malta in 60 CE while awaiting his transfer to Rome to stand trial. It's a small, damp and dull place, but its saintly association made this a pilgrimage site during the Knights' time. More recently, Pope Jean Paul II and Pope Benedict have both made a point of praying here during their visits to Malta, but today the site is more popular with tour groups than with pilgrims. Doubling back to the cave's entrance, staircases descend into a labyrinth of third-century

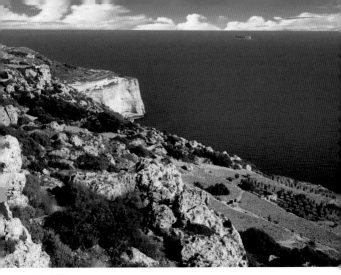

Dingli Cliffs

Roman catacombs (sadly looted over the centuries and quite devoid of artefacts) and World War II air raid shelters. The latter boast over fifty rooms that were hand dug to provide wartime refuge.

St Agatha's Catacombs

MAP P.66
Triq Sant Agata, Rabat ☎ 2145 9222. Mon–Fri 10am–5pm, Sat 10am–1pm. €5.
Located directly opposite St Paul's Catacombs, **St Agatha's** was in use from the Byzantine era (400 CE) through to the seventeenth century as a large burial complex of some four thousand square metres, of which only portions are publicly accessible. Also here is a crypt where St Agatha supposedly hid in 249 CE after she fled Roman persecution in Catania. Access to this atmospheric site is by guided tour only (every 30min, included in entrance fee), which begin at the crypt's two adjoining chapels. The smaller one is dedicated to the Madonna, while the larger chapel has several colourful ancient frescoes: the earliest three are exquisite Byzantine representations. Beyond the crypt, narrow rock-hewn tunnels of

tombs wind deep beneath Rabat's streets, including pre-Christian burial chambers complete with intact original skeletons, and later sixth-century Christian additions with frescoes rich in religious symbolism (shells represent heaven, pigeons: the soul, trees: life). An adjoining and disappointingly outdated museum presents a random assortment of historic artefacts, bones and religious paraphernalia.

Dingli Cliffs

MAP P.66, POCKET MAP D15
Triq Panoramika, Dingli. Bus #56 from Valletta.
This sweep of 250m-high chalky white limestone cliffs plummeting into the cobalt seas is a dizzyingly majestic sight. There are two spots for top views. The humble chapel of St Mary Magdalene, built in 1646, has benches dotted along the clifftop, where you can rest and contemplate Dingli's wild beauty. A pleasant 1.5km walk brings you to Ta Zuta, a headland criss-crossed with well-worn paths, which offers a more expansive view (plus the remains of a Bronze Age wall and silos).

Cafés

Fontanella Tea Gardens

MAP P.66

1 Pjazza Tas-Sur, Mdina ☏ 2145 0208. Daily: café 10am–7pm; wine bar 7pm–midnight.

With tables spread out over the parapet of the Mdina fortifications offering dreamy views over Malta, this is a great spot for afternoon tea and cake. It's even better at night, with the fortifications majestically lit and lights twinkling into the distance, when it morphs into a wine bar serving wine, other drinks and platters of finger-food.

Is-Serkin (Crystal Palace)

MAP P.66

90 Triq San Pawl, Rabat ☏ 2145 3323. Daily 4am–8pm.

An old-style joint, cluttered with Formica tables, offering some of Malta's best *pastizzi* – puff-pastry pockets stuffed with mushy peas or ricotta – as well as hot drinks and alcohol. Cheap and filling, and made with a lard-heavy dough, a couple of *pastizzi* are more than enough.

Palazzo de Piro

MAP P.66

3 Triq is-Sur, Mdina ☏ 2010 0560, ⓦ palazzo depiro.com. Daily 9.30am–10.30pm.

Set within a private sixteenth-century home built by Girolamo Cassar (who also designed St John's Co-Cathedral, the Grand Master's Palace and Auberge de Castille), *Palazzo de Piro* offers a light lunch menu of salads (€12) and sandwiches (€5–8). For a casual sunset dinner, try the homemade pasta (€12) or fried rabbit (€16).

Restaurants

De Mondion

MAP P.66

Mistrah il-Kunsill, Mdina ☏ 2145 0560, ⓦ xarapalace.com.mt. Daily 7.30–10.30pm.

Part of the five-star *Xara Palace* hotel, *De Mondion* is perhaps Malta's most luxurious dining venue, serving lavish dishes such as lobster cannelloni with squid ink (€32) or local rabbit pan-seared *en brioche* with pumpkin, king oysters and carob-flavoured rabbit *jus* (€32). The views from its bastion terrace (open summer only) are outstanding.

Fork and Cork

MAP P.66

21 Telgha tas-Saqqajja, Rabat ☏ 7904 7043, ⓦ forkandwork.com.mt Mon–Sat 6.30–10.30pm.

Fork and Cork is especially romantic at night, when lights from Malta's southern villages twinkle on the horizon of its small terrace. The food here evokes fine dining but the atmosphere is never fussy. Its seasonal menu rarely disappoints: think rabbit and quail with local figs and radish (€10.5) and Maltese grey meagre fish with bean cassoulet (€22).

Palazzo de Piro

Central Malta

Attard, Balzan and Lija – collectively known as the "Three Villages" – are laidback, leafy places, as desirable today as they were when the Knights built country retreats here. Attard's San Anton Gardens – formerly part of a Grand Master's residence – are now Malta's largest and plushest public gardens. Other sites scattered around the villages, which can be seen in a half-day's exploration (there's just a kilometre between each centre), include elegant medieval parish churches, fine old townhouses towering over narrow alleyways and endless delightful Baroque architectural features. Beyond the Three Villages, places of interest include Palazzo Parisio, the swankiest palace open to the public, in the town of Naxxar; and neighbouring Mosta, which boasts one of Europe's largest domes.

Attard

MAP P.76, POCKET MAP E14

The focal point of a visit to **Attard** is **St Mary's Church** (daily 7–10am & 5–7pm; free), set in the compact, quiet and pedestrianized Pjazza Tommaso Dingli. Designed in 1613, the church is regarded as the finest Renaissance church in Malta. Five minutes' walk north, along Triq Il-Kbira and then Triq Sant' Anton, takes you to Attard's other notable sight, **San Anton Gardens**.

San Anton Gardens

MAP P.76, POCKET MAP E14

Triq Birbal, Attard ☎ 2149 3170. June–Sept 7am–7pm; Oct–May 7am–5pm. Free.

In 1623, the French Grand Master Antoine de Paule built **San Anton Palace** and its **garden** as his private retreat. Today, as the official residence of Malta's President, it is not open to the public. You can,

however, access the large garden, enclosed by high perimeter walls and still retaining the intimate feel of a private estate. The gardens are dotted with oaks, ficus, cypresses, fragrant citrus groves and mature, towering palms. Laid around a grid pattern of cobbled paths, each transverse intersection is decorated with a stone fountain home to turtles, ducks, swans and goldfish. Peacocks and friendly street cats also roam freely.

Ta Qali National Park & Farmers Market

MAP P.76

Ta Qali National Park, Attard. Park daily 10am–7pm. Market daily 7am–5pm. Bus #56 from Valletta, #202 from Sliema or #186 from Buġibba.

For most of the year, Ta Qali National Park (formerly a World War II RAF station) is not much more than a large dustbowl

Visiting central Malta

The Three Villages are served by bus #56 from Valletta. From Buġibba, the #186 passes through Mosta en route to the Three Villages, and buses #31 and #41–49 pass through Naxxar to Mosta's town centre.

Mosta Dome

frequented by joggers or football fans heading for the National Football Stadium within. Its real draw is the chaotic, ramshackle Farmers Market (busiest on Mondays and Thursdays), where you can buy produce directly from over thirty local farmers alongside Malta's chefs. By law, the produce sold here is the freshest in the country, harvested no more than 24 hours before sale.

Balzan

MAP P.76, POCKET MAP E14

Balzan lays claim to the seventeenth-century **Wignacourt Aqueduct**, built by the Knights to carry water from springs in Dingli and Rabat to Valletta. The aqueduct remained in use until the twentieth century and most of its arches survive today, with the bulk flanking a busy motorway. It's not worth going out of your way for but you're likely to catch a glimpse during a bus ride to Rabat or Mdina.

Lija

MAP P.76, POCKET MAP E14

Lija is an affluent residential neighbourhood that developed from the sixteenth to eighteenth centuries. To see the Three Villages at their most evocative, visit Triq Sant' Anton with its eighteenth-century townhouses (those dating from Malta's British period have rather English front gardens and bay windows) and Triq Sant' Andrija with its seventeenth-century examples. Northwest of Triq Sant' Andrija and west of the main church, a picturesque network of alleyways branches off the winding, bougainvillea-dotted streets. Lija's main square, Misrah It-Trasfigurazzjoni, is dominated by its 1690s parish church. The square sees one of the best pyrotechnic shows in the world during the town feast each August.

Mosta Dome

MAP P.76, POCKET MAP D14

Triq il-Kbira, Mosta. Mon–Sat 9am–11.45am & 3–5pm. Free. Buses #31, #41, #42, #44, #45, #47, #48 and #260 from Valletta. Bus #202 from Sliema and #280 from Buġibba.

The nineteenth-century parish church of Santa Marija, better known as the **Mosta Dome**, deserves its place on Malta's tourist trail. Visible from vantage points all around the island, the huge rotunda – claimed to be Europe's third-largest – is unlike any other in Malta, designed by architect Georges Grognet de Vasse after the Pantheon. The sacristy is dedicated to recounting the "Miracle of St Mary" when, during World War II, a Luftwaffe bomb pierced the dome during Mass and skittered along the floor without exploding.

Palazzo Parisio

MAP P.76
29 Misraħ ir-Rebħa, Naxxar
Ⓦ palazzoparisio.com. Mon, Tues & Sun 9am–6pm, Wed–Sat 9am–11pm. €12. Buses #46, #49, #238 and #260 from Valletta, #203 from Sliema or Buġibba.
This nineteenth-century palace – sole draw of the town of Naxxar – is Malta's most opulent aristocratic home, a fantastic and overwhelming construction of

Study at the Palazzo Parisio

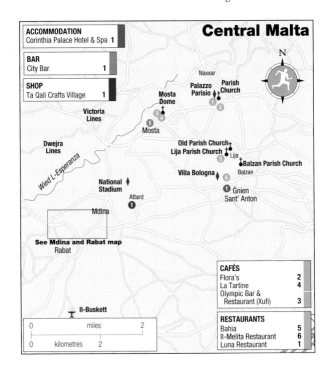

Central Malta

ACCOMMODATION
Corinthia Palace Hotel & Spa 1

BAR
City Bar 1

SHOP
Ta Qali Crafts Village 1

Naxxar
Palazzo Parisio — Parish Church
Mosta Dome
Victoria Lines
Mosta
Dwejra Lines
Wied L-Esperanza
Old Parish Church
Lija Parish Church — Lija
Balzan Parish Church
Villa Bologna — Balzan
National Stadium
Attard
Ġnien Sant' Anton
Mdina

See Mdina and Rabat map
Rabat

Il-Buskett

0 —— miles —— 2
0 —— kilometres —— 2

CAFÉS
Flora's 2
La Tartine 4
Olympic Bar & Restaurant (Xufi) 3

RESTAURANTS
Bahia 5
Il-Melita Restaurant 6
Luna Restaurant 1

frothy plasterwork reminiscent of a tiny Versailles. Built in the early eighteenth century as a hunting lodge by Portuguese Grand Master Manoel de Vilhena, the palace underwent an extravagant upgrade after Marquis Giuseppe Scicluna acquired it in 1898. Its interior seems plucked out of a fairytale; the Italian artist Filippo Venuti was commissioned to execute the paintings that decorate each room, and gilded Rococo-style stucco carvings blaze across the palace's walls, reaching a garish intensity in the ballroom. After touring the house you can explore the grounds, a green splash of lawns and fountains reminiscent of a British stately home's garden.

Il-Buskett and Verdala Palace

MAP P.76, POCKET MAP D15
Triq Il-Buskett, Il Buskett. Bus #81 from Valletta and Rabat.
Malta's only mature, self-generating woodland, **Il-Buskett** makes a good spot for a stroll or picnic. Created by the Knights in the seventeenth century, Il-Buskett served as the private hunting grounds of Verdala Palace, which was commissioned in 1586 by Grand Master Hugues Loubenx de Verdalle as a country retreat. The palace itself is closed to the public, though you can get a glimpse of its turreted exterior rising above the grove of Aleppo pines that surround it. The woodlands are reached via a snaking road immediately west of the palace, which ends at a car park, from where paths branch in different directions (there are no maps or formal trails). In the peak of summer it's better to give Buskett a miss, as the woodland becomes parched, dusty and punishingly hot. There are no facilities here so bring your own water and snacks.

Dingli Cliffs and Clapham Junction cart ruts

MAP P.76, POCKET MAP D15
Siġġiewi. Bus #62 from Valletta.
Named by British archaeologists after the similarly intricate web of railway lines at Clapham Junction station in London, this jumble of parallel grooves cut into a rocky plateau is the densest network of such ruts in Malta (similar channels are found all over the Mediterranean, but are most numerous here). Archaeologists are unable to date Malta's cart ruts or explain their use. The most accepted – although hazy – hypothesis is that they were made by wheeled carts during the Bronze Age (2000–1400 BC). However, the ruts have no apparent destination or pattern, disappearing into the sea or halting at cliff-edges. Even the tiny islet of Filfla (see page 101) is webbed with them. The debate on their date and origin continues, with explanations ranging from the simple (they were water channels) to the bizarre (they were made by aliens).

Cart ruts at Misrah Ghar il-Kbir

Shop

Ta Qali Crafts Village

MAP P.76

Vjal L-Istadium Nazzjonali, Ta Qali. Hours vary. Bus #80 from Valletta, #65 from Sliema or #66 from Buġibba.

The Maltese traditional crafts sold here are produced in the on-site workshops – many housed in former airplane hangars – and range from ceramics to jewellery. Mdina Glass (☎2141 5786; Mon–Fri 9am–5pm, Sat 9am–3pm) is the highlight of any visit, with free glass-blowing demonstrations. Note, though, that prices overall are lower at the Dbieġi Crafts Village in Gozo (see page 119).

Cafés

Flora's

MAP P.76

1 Misraħ ir-Rebħa, Naxxar ☎2141 0020. Mon–Fri 9am–9pm, Sat 9am–8pm, Sun 9am–1pm & 4–8pm.

A positively adorable, sun-drenched tea room with vintage style, *Flora's* specialises in afternoon

tea and cupcakes, and also offers consistently good breakfast and lunch options.

La Tartine

MAP P.76

11 Pjazza Rotunda, Mosta ☎2713 7800. Daily 8am–9pm.

A French café serving authentic and affordable French pastries, as well as the requisite Maltese pastas and sandwiches. The *jambon beurre* with smoked ham and pickle (€4.50), *croque monsieurs* (€4) and French cheese platter with baguette (€10) are sure bets.

Olympic Bar & Restaurant (Xufi)

MAP P.76

Triq il-Kostituzzjoni, Mosta ☎2155 7232. Mon–Fri & Sun 5am–5.30pm, Sat 5am–midnight.

Jam-packed with locals enjoying huge portions of rustic Maltese food plus lots of chatter and banter, the Olympic (more commonly called *Xufi*, the owner's nickname, by locals) is famous for its *ftira* (a roundish ciabatta filled to your liking with tomatoes, cheese, sausage, hard boiled eggs, onions

Ta Qali Crafts Village

Luna The Restaurant

and olives), acknowledged as some of the best in Malta.

Restaurants

Bahia

MAP P.76

75 Triq Preziosi, Lija ☏ 9999 1270, ⓦ bahia.com.mt. Tues–Sun 7–11pm.
Bahia preserves local culinary traditions and (too often overlooked) local ingredients with a seasonal twelve-item menu of flawless old-meets-new dishes. Expect delicacies such as local stone bass *sous vide* in olive oil with heirloom tomatoes (€22), or lamb with *ras el hanout* couscous, homemade falafel and wild-fennel-roasted potatoes (€27).

Il-Melita Restaurant

MAP P.76

Triq Birbal, Balzan ☏ 2147 0663. Daily 10am–11pm.
A big family-friendly restaurant offering an array of inexpensive meals such as pies, baguettes, pasta, pizza (€8) and even English breakfasts (€7; served until 6pm). It's most pleasant to visit during fine weather, when ample seating is offered in the restaurant's large garden that abuts San Anton Gardens.

Luna The Restaurant

MAP P.76

28 Misraħ ir-Rebħa, Naxxar ☏ 2141 2461, ⓦ palazzoparisio.com. Daily 9am–late, afternoon tea 3–6pm.
Located in the extravagant *Palazzo Parisio*, Malta's very own miniature Versaille, the suitably luxurious *Luna* is best known for its afternoon tea service (€35). The next best time to visit is for lunch – opt for a table outside to enjoy a classic coronation chicken salad (€15) or breaded veal Milanese (€26) in view of the palace's fragrant gardens.

Bar

City Bar

MAP P.76

Triq il-Kbira, Mosta ☏ 2143 2080. Mon & Tues 10.30am–2.30pm & 5.30pm–1am, Wed–Sun 10am–2.30pm & 5.30pm–1am.
A popular, quirky pub located just off Mosta's main square, this fifty-year-old institution offers reliably cheap drinks, always served with free snacks. Owing to its massive popularity with locals of all ages, the pub frequently hosts special events from live music to poetry readings.

The north

The north is the least densely populated area of Malta, characterised by a series of ridges and wide, fertile valleys. Inexpensive accommodation is one draw, particularly in resort town Buġibba; others include the region's multitude of small sandy beaches and family attractions like the Malta Aquarium (see page 82). Development is sparser in Mellieħa, a pleasant, airy town that is the best base in this part of Malta. St Paul's Bay, meanwhile, can refer – confusingly – to both the village of St Paul's Bay and the region that envelops the villages of Buġibba, Qawra and Xemxija. The name is derived from the legend that Saint Paul was shipwrecked on one of the little isles situated nearby. The Knights built a number of watchtowers in the area, including Wignacourt Tower, the oldest surviving watchtower in Malta, but it was not until after World War II that development in this area began in earnest, giving the northern villages their mid-century modern charm.

Buġibba

MAP P.84, F11–G11

Built up in the 1970s as a
resort for sun-and-sea package
tourism, **Buġibba** is blighted by
poor planning and hotchpotch
development. The back-to-back
apartment blocks and mid-range
hotels are dense and dull, but a
select few residential streets will
transport you back in time with
their pretty pastel townhouses
and geometric concrete balconies.
Cheap rents have resulted in an
increasing number of affordable
self-catered accommodation and
the inexpensive hotels continue to
do brisk business, making Buġibba
extremely popular amongst
retired British expats, young
clubbers, and tourists visiting for
hen and stag dos. Given its good
public transport connections and
abundance of restaurants and bars,
Buġibba is a viable and convenient

National Aquarium

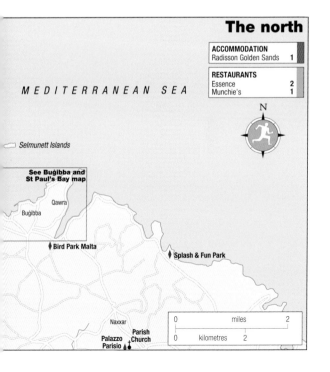

The north

ACCOMMODATION	
Radisson Golden Sands	1

RESTAURANTS	
Essence	2
Munchie's	1

MEDITERRANEAN SEA

N

Selmunett Islands

**See Buġibba and
St Paul's Bay map**

Qawra

Buġibba

♦ Bird Park Malta

♦ Splash & Fun Park

Naxxar

Parish
Church

Palazzo
Parisio

0	miles	2
0	kilometres	2

Visiting the north

Transport connections to the north are good, but expect at least a 40min ride to Sliema and Valletta. Direct services to Malta's main sights run from Buġibba's tourist-oriented bus station on Triq It-Turisti. From Buġibba, bus routes follow the coast north or south, or venture inland towards Mosta and Malta's fertile valleys. The main routes are #58 to Valletta; #221 to Ċirkewwa via St Paul's Bay and Mellieħa; #212 & 225 to Sliema via St Julian's; #223 & 250 to Għajn Tuffieħa and Golden Bay beaches via St Paul's Bay; #186 to Rabat and Mdina; #427 to Marsaxlokk via Tarxien; and #X3 from the airport directly to Buġibba. All buses to Mellieħa pass through St Paul's Bay town centre.

From Valletta, routes #41 and #42 pass through Buġibba and Mellieħa, terminating at Ċirkewwa. #X1 runs from Ċirkewwa through Mellieħa and Buġibba to the airport. All buses bound for Ċirkewwa also pass Għadira Bay beach, Għadira Wetland, the Red Tower and Paradise Bay.

All these services wind down by 11 pm, and afterwards a special night service (#N11) operates from Paċeville to Buġibba, Mellieħa and Ċirkewwa until 4am.

base – but you'll want to spend the bulk of your time elsewhere.

The town's action is mostly concentrated in and around Triq It-Turisti, which is full of tour operators offering excursions round the islands, and the nearby Bay Square (Misraħ Il-Bajja), a small, lively pedestrianized plaza fringed by bars, restaurants and cafés.

Qawra

MAP P.84, POCKET MAP G10–H11

Like its bigger sister Buġibba, Qawra is replete with inexpensive, multi-storey three star hotels, but has fewer bars and restaurants to recommend it. However, the northeastern tip of its shoreline is lined with candy-coloured 1960s villas and boat houses that are worth a quick detour.

National Aquarium

MAP P.84, POCKET MAP H10
Triq it-Trunciera, Qawra ☎ 2248 8100, ⓦ aquarium.com.mt. Daily 10am–8pm. €13–6. Bus #45 from Valletta and #212, #222 or #225 from Sliema
Malta's new **National Aquarium**, housed in a beautiful star-fish-shaped building is (like most

attractions on the island) compact but compelling. The highlight is the tunnel tank, where horn sharks, dragon eels and cownose rays swim overhead. There are also tanks featuring local fish, with informative displays to help you identify species commonly spotted while snorkelling and swimming off Malta's shores, such as sea bream, sea bass, mullet, grouper, amberjacks and scorpionfish. A baby station, where different species of fish are bred, is endlessly fascinating – visitors can see eggs and embryos of dogfish, seahorses and sometimes sharks. There are also tropical tanks with puffer fish and clown fish, and a reptiles and amphibians area. The on-site restaurant offers good lunch and dinner options.

Classic Car Museum

MAP P.84, POCKET MAP G11
Tourists Street, Qawra ☎ 2157 8885, ⓦ classiccarsmalta.com. Mon–Fri 9am–6pm, Sat 9am–1.30pm. €4.50–9. Bus #45 from Valletta and buses #212, #222 and #225 from Sliema
This 3000-square-metre private museum presents a line-up of

pristinely restored T-Birds, Spitfires, Fiats, Alfas, MGs, Jaguars, Fords and other models, alongside antiques and memorabilia from the 1940s to 60s, including typewriters, gramophones, model toys and period clothes. Restorations are often done live on site in the museum's workshop.

Bird Park Malta

MAP P.80

Triq l-Imdawra, Burmarrad ☎ 9986 8608, ⓦ birdparkmalta.com. Tues–Fri 10am–3pm, Sat & Sun 10am–5pm. €5–8. Bus #49 from Valletta and #212, #222 or #225 from Sliema

Little **Bird Park Malta** is home to over two hundred species of birds and animals, including kangaroos, wallabies, deer, snakes and goats. The highlight of any visit – particularly if cages are not your thing – is the small lagoon, home to dozens of pink flamingos (wild flamingos are known to rest here during their annual migrations). The on-site café is best avoided.

St Paul's Bay

MAP P.84, POCKET MAP F11

Follow Buġibba's seaside promenade northwest and you'll encounter **St Paul's Bay village**, with its ribbon of development skirting the coast. Originally a small fishing village, it's tourism that now holds sway here, though the small remaining fleet lends it a picturesque aspect. The seaside promenade is particularly lovely, dotted with towering palm trees.

Wignacourt Tower

MAP P.84, POCKET MAP F11

Tower Road, Buġibba ☎ 2122 5952, ⓦ dinlarthelwa.org. Mon–Sat 10am–1pm. €2. Buses #41, #42 and #49 from Valletta

Built in 1609 to guard the entrance into St Paul's Bay, **Wignacourt Tower** is one of the largest of the defensive chain built around Malta's coastline by the Knights. A squarish, boxy design, its walls rising solidly to four partly embedded corner turrets, the tower now holds an interesting exhibition that illustrates the Knights' military architecture in Malta with prints of the designs and models of some of the varied defence structures scattered throughout the islands. The first floor re-creates the living quarters of the *capomastro* (master bombardier), who was in charge

Classic Car Museum

St Paul's shipwreck

The history of St Paul's Bay is firmly rooted in the story of the saint himself, whom Christians believe was shipwrecked here during his voyage to Rome to stand trial for heresy in 60 AD. To date, no archaeological evidence of the saint's shipwreck has been uncovered. In 2005, a diver discovered a one-tonne lead anchor of the right age and origin in St Paul's Bay, but researchers have been unable to link this anchor to the actual vessel the saint was shipwrecked on, nor have they found any archaeological candidates for the vessel itself. There is also debate over whether, if he did land in Malta, it was in St Paul's Bay or at one of dozens of similar inlets in Malta. Regardless, legend has it that proof of St Paul's miraculous abilities came after he survived a snakebite – Maltese snakes ceased to be venomous thereafter – and he then spent three months converting the Maltese population to Christianity. St Paul's story is now embedded in the national ethos, with the date of the shipwreck, February 10, a national holiday.

A huge statue of St Paul, easily spotted from surrounding villages, dominates the largest of St Paul's Islands, two offshore islets where St Paul's galley supposedly smashed into the rocks. The statue, financed by a local merchant in 1845, depicts St Paul trampling on a snake and brandishing the Bible. Both of the islands are nature reserves dedicated to the protection of a subspecies of the Maltese lizard and Malta's last community of pure wild rabbits.

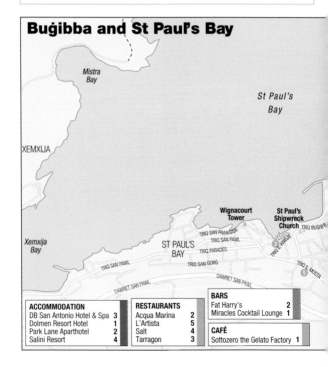

of the tower with the assistance of two gunners. The soldiers led a plain, rather monastic life here, as evidenced by the undecorated bed, table and benches, and the stone cooking hearth. A staircase leads to the roof, where one of the two original cannons survive, and which affords a lovely view that takes in the entire sweep of St Paul's Bay.

Mistra Bay

MAP P.84, POCKET MAP D10–E11
Buses #41, #42 and #49 from Valletta.
Scenically located at the mouth of a valley that steps up on either side to picturesque terraced fields, horseshoe-shaped **Mistra Bay** is a nice spot for a stroll by the sea. There are no sandy beaches anywhere in the environs of St Paul's Bay and this bay is no different, its shore consisting of a strip of pebbles backed by an access road. The bay is a favourite place for anglers, and on its southern

Mistra Bay

flank a path leads up from the shoreline to a bluff where heaps of boulders tumble down to a clear sea; if you can negotiate getting in and out of the water here you'll be rewarded with good

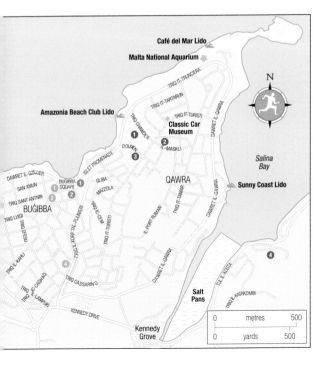

Lidos

The sea around Buġibba and Qawra is clean and clear, but the rocky coast isn't very comfortable for sunbathing. Your best bet is to head to one of the nearby **lidos**, the best of which is **Café del Mar** in Qawra (April–Oct, daily 10am–late), a splendid modern complex with an infinity pool overlooking the sea, an on-site restaurant offering excellent salads and pizzas, and a fully stocked bar with sunbed service. Entrance here will set you back €15–30 per person, depending on the quality of sunbed you opt for, but drink and food prices are surprisingly affordable. A larger and cheaper option is **Amazonia Beach Club** on Buġibba's seafront (May–Oct daily 9am–6pm; €12 on weekdays, €15 at weekends), which has a pool, café and bar, and a nightclub that starts at 10pm. Sunny Coast Resort in Qawra, meanwhile, also offers day passes to its seaview pool (daily 9am–7pm; €12 Mon–Sat, €17 Sun).

snorkelling among the rocky boulders that string the coast. The impeccably preserved eighteenth-century Mistra Battery sits on the bay's northern flank. Built by the Knights, today it's closed to the public for restoration works, though a short walk around its perimeter walls is worthwhile. The best time to visit is in the spring; in the height of summer a blight of motorhomes line the access road, effectively blocking beach access.

Mellieħa Church Complex

Mellieħa

MAP P.89, POCKET MAP C13
Buses #41 and #42 from Valletta, #222 from Sliema and #221 from Buġibba.
Spread over the Mellieħa Ridge, **Mellieħa** has only recently developed any kind of a resort ethic. The fringes of the largely anonymous residential sprawl now bear a peppering of holiday apartments and exclusive villas that cling to its slopes and cliffs, spilling down towards Mellieħa Bay. The narrow, sloping Triq Ġorġ Borg Olivier defines the town centre and holds a smorgasbord of small shops and restaurants. At its northern extremity, Triq Ġorġ Borg Olivier gives way to Triq Il-Marfa, the main artery that snakes down the slope to Mellieħa Bay before cutting across the Marfa Ridge all the way to Ċirkewwa (for the Gozo ferry).

Mellieħa Church Complex

MAP P.89
Parish Square, Mellieħa. Buses #41 and #42 from Valletta, #222 from Sliema and #221 from Buġibba.
Mellieħa's two **churches** sit atop each other at the edge of the Mellieħa Ridge, overlooking Mellieħa Bay. The older of the two is set in the Sanctuary, a lovely courtyard that's accessible from the square (Misraħ Iż-Żjara Tal-

Grotto of Our Lady

Papa) via the Monumental Arch, a Baroque stone archway built in 1716. The courtyard is flanked on the right by simple rooms built in the eighteenth century to house pilgrims, and on the left by the **Church of Our Lady of Mellieħa** (daily: June–Sept 8am–noon & 5–7pm; Oct–May 8am–noon & 4–6pm; free). A squat structure embedded into the rockface, the church began as a crypt and has been expanded twice since the sixteenth century to accommodate the increasing number of pilgrims drawn to the fresco atop the altar, depicting the Madonna cradling Jesus in her arms and said to have been painted by St Luke in 60 AD. The clutter of votive offerings lining the tunnel into the church illustrate the continued belief in the fresco's healing powers, though recent studies have indicated that the saint may not have painted it.

Opposite the Monumental Arch, a second archway and staircase leads up to the bluff that the larger and newer **Mellieħa Parish Church** (daily 6–8.30am & 5–7.30pm; free) stands on. Built in the mid-nineteenth century to

accommodate the town's growing population, its lean pyramidal dome and bell towers, and its setting at the edge of the ridge, make it a dramatic feature of the skyline. The interior, a bare stone affair with floral carved Baroque motifs, is elegant in its restraint.

Grotto of Our Lady

MAP P.89
94 Ġorġ Borg Olivier St, Mellieħa. Daily 8am–6pm (winter) & 8am–7pm (summer). Free.
Across the road from the Sanctuary, a small unmarked doorway from Triq Ġorġ Borg Olivier opens onto a staircase that cuts through an ivy-clogged little valley to the rock-cut chapel known as the **Grotto of Our Lady**, which has existed since medieval times. The only decoration under the softly curved roof is an unremarkable statue of the Madonna enclosed by a metal grille, with a pond fed by an underground spring at its foot; both are said to have miraculous healing powers. Many still have faith in the redemptive properties, as evidenced by the candles left by believers, and the votive offerings nailed to the walls.

The Red Tower

Air raid shelter

MAP P.89
Our Lady of the Grotto Street, Mellieħa.
Mon–Sat 9am–3.30pm. €2. Bus #41 and
#42 from Valletta, #222 from Sliema and
#221 from Buġibba.

Dug to protect Mellieħa's population during World War II air raids, the town's 500m of underground rooms and tunnels have been opened up as a fascinating, somewhat eerie attraction. Excavated by hand to accommodate upwards of 3000 people, this is one of the largest of such networks in Malta. Some of the rooms are kitted out with mannequins and furniture, giving a tangible impression of the realities of war here.

Għadira Bay Beach

MAP P.80

Għadira Bay, a 300m-long stretch of sand lapped by water that is ankle-deep for some 50m out to sea, is Malta's busiest beach. There's parking galore (a main road runs parallel) and good facilities including watersports equipment for rent and a top-notch restaurant. The beach is at its most magical at sunset, when the skyline of Mellieħa is illuminated by twinkling festoons of lights.

The Red Tower

MAP P.80, POCKET MAP C13
Triq tad-Dahar, Mellieħa ☏ 2122 5952.
Daily: June–Sept 10am–1pm and 3–6pm;
Oct–May 10am–4pm, or when the flag is
flying. €2. Bus #41 and #42 from Valletta.

The **Red Tower**, erected in 1649 to supplement the defence afforded by Wignacourt Tower, is colloquially named for the dried-blood colour of its paint job (its formal name is St Agatha's Tower). The tower cuts an imposing, rather fairy-tale figure on the Marfa Ridge, a rugged crest of garigue (a rocky habitat of herbaceous and hardy bushes) interspersed by groves of trees planted during a 1970s reforestation drive. The tower is a boxy construction with outer walls 4m thick, and four mini-towers at each corner. The Knights fitted it with cannons and stationed a brigade of 49 soldiers here, making it the main point of defence in this part of Malta. It was later used by the British as a signalling station during World War II. It's now open to the public, with a short film and somewhat dry informative panels.

Ras Il-Qammiegħ

MAP P.80
Bus #41 and #42 from Valletta.

Beyond the Red Tower, the narrow road that continues west along the crest of the ridge makes for an excellent walk or drive, with wonderful views on either side. Dotted with the stone huts of bird-trappers and hunters, the windswept, scrubby landscape is fragrant with wild thyme, whose light-purple flowers bloom in late spring (peaking in June). At the head of the ridge, the **Ras Il-**

Qammiegh cliffs plummet down dramatically; at the base, boulders as large as churches tumble towards the sea.

Paradise Bay

MAP P.80, POCKET MAP C12
Bus #41 or #42 from Valletta, #222 from Sliema and #221 from Buġibba.
Paradise Bay, a cream-coloured little stretch of sand snuggled into an inlet, is the most attractive of all the Marfa Ridge peninsula's beaches, with clear waters that offer good snorkelling. There are sunbeds, umbrellas and kayaks to rent, a car park, and a bar for refreshments.

Popeye's Village

MAP P.80
Triq Tal-Prajjet, Mellieħa ☎ 2152 4782, Ⓦ popeyemalta.com. Daily: Nov–Mar, 9.30am–4.30pm; Apr–Jun & Sep–Oct, 9.30am–5.30pm; Jul–Aug, 9.30am–7pm. Adults €14.50, children €11.50.

The 1980 Hollywood film, *Popeye*, starring Robin Williams, was shot almost entirely in Malta at a purpose-built set – a jumble of colourful buildings overlooking little Anchor Bay – that is now a tourist attraction. Families can make a day of it playing minigolf, visiting the comic book museum and meeting animators dressed as movie characters. In the summer, free boat trips are offered around the bay, which is lined with sunbeds for parents and floating bouncy castles for tots.

Ġnejna Bay

MAP P.80
Bus #44 from Valletta and #225 from Sliema and Buġibba; transfer to bus #101 at Mellieħa.

Beyond Mġarr (a small, uninteresting town founded in the nineteenth century) the road continues to **Ġnejna Bay**, a large scenic bay nestled in a trough at the

Mellieħa

ACCOMMODATION	
Maritim Antonine	1
Splendid Guest House	2

RESTAURANTS	
The Arches	3
Bouquet Garni	4
Commando	2
il-Mithna	5
One80 Kitchen & Lounge	1
Rebekah's	6

BARS	
Charlie's Bar	1
Crosskeys	2

Mellieħa Parish Church
THE SANCTUARY OF ST PAUL
Church of Our Lady of Mellieħa
Air raid shelter
Grotto of Our Lady

N

0 metres 200
0 yards 200

mouth of a valley. The small swath of orange-coloured sand backed by clear, calm water is popular with local families in summer, and mostly undiscovered by tourists. The bay itself is enclosed by dramatic clay slopes crowned by craggy amber cliffs; at the highest vantage point stands one of the Knights' seventeenth-century coastal defence towers.

Għajn Tuffieħa and Golden Bay

MAP P.80, POCKET MAP C13
Bus #44 from Valletta and #225 from Sliema and Buġibba.

North of Ġnejna Bay lie Malta's most scenic sandy beaches, divided by a gently rounded peninsula. The southerly of the two, **Għajn Tuffieħa**, is the more dramatic, with the typical clay slopes and cliffs of the coastal landscape hereabouts. A long flight of stairs from the clifftop car park leads to the narrow, crescent-shaped beach, lapped by water that takes on the warm auburn colour of the seabed. During the winter, this is one of the only beaches where surfing is possible; in the summer, the sea is calm and azure. **Golden Bay** is partly spoiled by a multi-storey hotel that dominates the bay from its clifftop perch and, nearer the sand, the road and car park that reach down to the beach. This easier access also means it gets more crowded than Għajn Tuffieħa in summer.

Park il-Majjistral

MAP P.80
Triq Għajn Tuffieħa, Manikata ☎ 2152 1291, ⓦ majjistral.org. Free. Bus #44 from Valletta and #225 from Sliema & Buġibba.

Stretching 6km from the coastal area at Golden Bay beach, **Park il-Majjistral** (Majjistral Nature and History Park) offers excellent gentle hiking, with picturesque views of countryside, cliff and ocean. The park is home to a spectacular diversity of local flora and fauna, including olive and carob trees, myrtle, rockrose and golden samphire. Some 430 different plant species – almost half of the plants known in the whole of Malta – have been recorded to date. Hedgehogs, wild rabbits, Mediterranean chameleons, sparrows and warblers may also be spotted amongst the garigue habitat. On the manmade side of things, you're also likely to encounter remnants of corbelled stone huts (called *giren),* cart ruts, rubble walls, and entrenchments built as part of a coastal defence system by the Knights in the early eighteenth century. Of more recent origin are the WWII pillboxes, a British military barracks and a disused shooting range. The park is most easily accessed through the path that winds behind the *Radisson Blu Golden Sands* resort or by following the signs towards "Haxix Frisk" (fresh vegetables) on Triq in-Nahhalija. After the large dirt car park, turn left onto an unmarked road, where you'll pass a vegetable stand on your way to the park's interpretation centre (Mon–Sat 9am–3pm) that offers maps detailing five recommended walks. There are no facilities once you set off, so take your own water.

Splash & Fun Park

MAP P.80
Coast Road, Baħar iċ-Ċagħaq ☎ 2137 4283, ⓦ splashandfunmalta.com. May–Oct daily 9am–8pm. Adults €22, children €15; half-day and multi-day tickets available. Bus #13 from Valletta, #212, #222 and #225 from Sliema, and #222 from Buġibba.

Malta's only **water park** is small and quaint, but offers a pleasant place to spend a day with children. Attractions include a lazy river, a large wave pool, and several water slides including the "Sidewinder", "Kamikaze" and the 120m-long "Black Hole". The onsite pizzeria is slightly below average but affordable.

Café

Sottozero the Gelato Factory

MAP P.84

46 Triq Ir-Rebbiegħa, Buġibba ☎ 2701 9339, Ⓦ sottozerofactory.com. Daily 8am–1am.

The region's most popular gelato destination, serving traditional Italian flavours. Expect a queue, but it's worth the wait.

Restaurants

Acqua Marina

MAP P.84

160 St Anthony St, Buġibba ☎ 2703 4933. Daily 10.45am–11pm.

Run by a single family, this kitsch, nautical-themed restaurant is arguably the best Sicilian restaurant in all of Malta. If you speak a little Italian, ask your affable host Carlo (the family's elderly patriarch) to fix you a mix of whatever is best that day – expect a multi-course feast of well-priced *antipasti*, pasta, seafood salads, *caponata* and fresh cheeses to miraculously emerge from the restaurant's tiny kitchen (about €20 per person). Don't skimp on dessert – the deconstructed *cannoli* are divine.

The Arches

MAP P.89

113 George Borg Olivier St, Mellieħa ☎ 2152 3460, Ⓦ archesrestaurant. com.mt. Tues–Thurs 7–10pm, Fri & Sat 7–10.30pm.

A modern restaurant with classic touches, a beautiful wine cellar (housed in a glass-fronted cave) and French-inspired fusion dishes. The imaginative menu changes seasonally and may include chateaubriand steak (for two; €70) or pan-fried duck breast with wild berry *gastrique* and wilted bok choi (€24). If you can't choose, go for the five-course tasting menu (€45/person).

L'Artista

MAP P.84

14 Triq Il-Mosta, Buġibba ☎ 9995 4947, Ⓦ facebook.com/artistamalta. Wed–Sat 7.30–11pm, Sun 12.30–3.30pm & 7.30–11pm.

A fantastic Sardinian seafood restaurant off the beaten path. The owner is also host – follow his recommendations for a memorable evening.

Bouquet Garni

MAP P.89

4 Ġorġ Borg Olivier St, Mellieħa ☎ 2152 2234, Ⓦ facebook.com/bouquetgarnimalta. Mon–Sat 6–10pm.

This cosy restaurant has a near flawless reputation for good food, reasonable prices and warm hospitality. Fresh fish is a mainstay on the menu, and the octopus here is particularly good. Mains €14–21.

Commando

MAP P.89

1 Misraħ iz-Zjara tal Papa, Mellieħa ☎ 9949 8843, Ⓦ commandorestaurant.com. Tues–Sat 6–10.30pm, Sun noon–3.30pm.

A foodie favourite located in front of the picturesque Mellieħa parish

Mithna

One80 Kitchen & Lounge

ambience, and the terrace a larger, slightly more upscale menu. Both offer sweeping views and both menus are delicious, including the picante pizza with spicy chorizo sausage (€10), the home-made pumpkin ravioli (€13), and the generous seafood platter (€38 for two).

One80 Kitchen & Lounge

MAP P.89

30 Triq Il-Wied Ta' Ruman, Mellieħa ☎ 2152 1637, Ⓦ one80.com.mt. Mon–Thurs & Sun noon–10.30pm, Fri & Sat noon–11pm.
Located on the beautiful hill below Mellieħa's parish church, *One80* boasts 180-degree views of Mellieħa Bay. Lunch, early and late dinner are served daily with menus that offer a winning blend of comfort food and creativity – think *boullabaisse* arancini (€9) and pan-seared tuna salad with lemongrass and coriander salsa (€15).

Rebekah's

MAP P.89

12 Triq it-Tgham, Mellieħa ☎ 2152 1154, Ⓦ rebekahs.com.mt. Mon–Sat 7–10.30pm, Sunday noon–3pm (winter) or 7–10.30pm (summer).
Located on a quiet Mellieħa street in a beautifully restored house of character, *Rebekah's* offers a perfect taste of contemporary local cuisine and old-world charm. The pork cheeks, risottos, *tortellaci* and fresh fish are all top notch. The restaurant also graciously caters to vegetarian and gluten-free requests with food that is no less superb than the rest. Mains €10–28.

Salt

MAP P.84

Triq Il-Korp Tal-Pijunieri, Buġibba ☎ 2157 8004, Ⓦ salt.com.mt. Mon–Sat 7–10.30pm.
Run by a young Maltese chef/owner, who gained experience working abroad at Michelin-starred restaurants, *Salt* is a lively modern restaurant. Try the Moroccan octopus with parmesan ice cream, orange curd, truffle-infused jersey royal potatoes and pickled pear

church. *Commando* offers seasonal dishes such as local prawn carpaccio with cauliflower and prawn rice croquettes (€13) or grilled ribeye with porcini butter and polenta chips (€27).

Essence

MAP P.80

1 Misrah iz-Zjara tal Papa, Mellieħa ☎ 2356 1920. Tues–Sat 6pm–late.
This high-end restaurant, located at the Radisson Golden Sands resort, offers a French-Mediterranean fusion menu served in a beautiful setting atop Golden Bay beach. Mains €20–28.

Mithna

MAP P.89

58 Triq Il-Kbira, Mellieħa ☎ 2152 0404, Ⓦ mithna.com. Daily 6–10.30pm. Mains €13–30.
A popular Maltese-Italian restaurant offering excellent value for money. The goat's cheese crêpe with orange-soaked figs and beetroot (€10) and traditional slow-cooked pork belly (€20) are recommended.

Munchie's

MAP P.80

Marfa Road, Mellieħa ☎ 2157 6416, Ⓦ munchies.com.mt. Daily 11am–11pm.
Malta's best beachside restaurant, *Munchie's* is split over two levels: the lower level offers a casual menu and

(€13) or 72-hour fenugreek pork belly with local black pudding, roasted apple vanilla purée and spiced Madeira wine jus (€22).

Tarragon

MAP P.84

Church St, St Paul's Bay ☎ 2157 3759, ⓦtarragonmalta.com. Mon–Fri 6.30–11pm, Sat 6.30pm–12.30am, Sun 12–3.30pm & 6.30–11pm.

By one of Malta's most renowned chefs, *Tarragon* offers Mediterranean fare with a firmly modern twist at surprisingly good prices. Indulge with cold foie gras pate bonbons dipped in chocolate and hazelnuts (€13) or venison and pistachio ravioli tossed in honey and coffee crème fraiche (€18).

Bars

Charlie's Bar

MAP P.89

Triq il-Hasira, Mellieha ☎ 2152 2010. Tues–Sun noon–midnight.

A quirky British-run hole in the wall where the drinks are cheap and the crowd is cheerful. Cards and board games are made available, and there's even a small swimming pool. Bingo nights are hosted on Tuesdays (book ahead).

Crosskeys

MAP P.89

5 Cross Square, Mellieha ☎ 2152 3744. Wed–Sun 6–11pm.

Despite its rather dated decor, *Crosskeys* is very popular with locals, British expats and tourists. British-style roasts are available on Sundays.

Fat Harry's

MAP P.84

Pjazza Walkway, Buġibba ☎ 2157 2163. Daily 11am–11.30pm.

Located just off Buġibba's main square, *Fat Harry's* makes a decent stab at authentic pub decor and offers a fantastic atmosphere, plus a varied menu of pub grub and drinks.

Miracles Cocktail Lounge

MAP P.84

Bay Square, Buġibba ☎ 99689017, ⓦmiracleslounge.com.

A very popular lounge bar on Buġibba's lively main square serving cocktails by the glass (€6) or pitcher (€17) alongside sharing platters (€20–27) and burgers (€10). Miracles shows major sports matches and has extensive outdoor seating.

Essence

THE NORTH

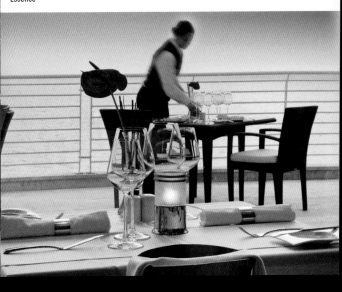

The south

Malta's least-touristy region consists of a clutch of old towns and seaside villages that have retained a measure of traditional Maltese life now absent from the more commercial north. Most distinctive are Żejtun and Marsascala. The former is a self-possessed old-style town whose charm comes mostly from its atmosphere, although it does also have an exceptional church. The latter is a sleepy seaside village that has largely escaped the development of resorts and high rises, and has a lovely seaside promenade and rocky beach to recommend it. Undoubtedly the most famous village in the south is Marsaxlokk, where a daily open-air market draws crowds to purchase fish fresh from the traditional, brightly painted luzzu boats moored nearby.

The south is also home to a few small beaches and Malta's finest four **Neolithic temples**, all World Heritage Sites, ranging from the underground Hypogeum to the enormous temples set atop tumbling coastal cliffs near Wied Iż-Żurrieq. **Accommodation** options in the South are limited to self-serviced apartments, so most

visitors chose to stay in Valletta, Sliema/St Julian's or Buġibba and venture south for day-trips.

Tarxien Neolithic temples

MAP P.96, POCKET MAP E15–G15
Triq it-Templi Neolitici, Tarxien ☎ 2169 5578, ⦵ heritagemalta.org. Daily 9am–5pm. €6. Buses #82, #84, #85 and #88 from Valletta.

The largest and most architecturally advanced temple complex in Malta, the **Tarxien Neolithic temples** are among the last built on the island, some time between 3000 and 2500 BCE. Evidence of fires here suggests that Bronze Age people used the buildings as a crematorium. For millennia the complex lay buried under an accumulation of rubble until it was discovered by a farmer in 1914. What survives now is the bottom third of the temples; the building, when intact, stood some 23m high. The Tarxien complex comprises three interlinked temples. Entry is through the South Temple, where the first chamber holds a grand altar with spiral reliefs and a replica of the bottom half of Malta's iconic "fat lady" sculpture (the original is in the National

Tarxien Neolithic temples

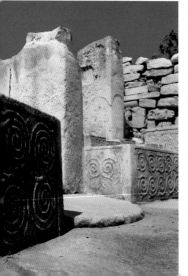

Museum of Archaeology; see page 33). When whole, it would have measured 2.5m high, making this the largest of these figures found anywhere in the world. The Central Temple's symmetrical chambers contain evidence of arched roofing, and if you look closely at a chamber to the right you can see faded but breathtaking motifs of marching bulls and goats carved on the megaliths. Only a bottom foundation stone survives of the East Temple, but a number of altars found here (now at the National Museum of Archaeology) contained flint knife and animal bones, meaning animal sacrifices probably took place here.

Ħal Saflieni Hypogeum

MAP P.96, POCKET MAP E15
Triq iċ-Ċimiterju, Paola ☎ 2180 5019,
🌐 heritagemalta.org. Daily 9am–4pm.
€35. Buses #82, #84, #85 and #88 from Valletta.

The **Ħal Saflieni Hypogeum** is one of the oldest and most impressive monuments of the ancient world. This extensive underground shrine was cut into soft globigerina limestone over three levels between 3600 and 2500 BCE, and was still a work in progress when Malta's Neolithic settlers disappeared without trace. It was only rediscovered in 1899, and today the full purpose of the Hypogeum remains a matter of conjecture and debate. It was certainly connected to funerary ritual, but the fact that only seven thousand bodies were recovered here – which means just seven burials per year over the thousand years the Hypogeum was in use – suggests that only priests or

Ħal Saflieni Hypogeum

priestesses were laid to rest here. Whatever the Hypogeum's exact function, it's a unique structure with a tangible air of mystery, and you really do have to see it to appreciate its profoundly stirring atmosphere.

45-minute **tours** of the complex start with an audiovisual presentation, and proceed with an audio-guide tour supervised by watchful tour guides. You begin on the first (and oldest) level, where an intact entrance trilithon (two upright megaliths with another laid on top) creates a gateway into the underground realm. Archaeologists believe the second and most ornate level is where funerary processions began. It is daubed with spiral representations in evocative red ochre, perhaps representing the Neolithic people's world-view of cyclical continuity. An incomplete

Visiting the south

The attractions in the south are fairly scattered but can be reached by bus. Routes #80–94 (most depart from Valletta) service the south via Marsaxlokk, Tarxien and Żejtun. After 11pm, the #N10 night bus runs from Paċeville to Marsascala and Żejtun until 4am.

Visiting the Hypogeum

Only eighty people are allowed in each day so visits need to be planned well ahead – bookings (through ⓦ heritagemalta.com) are often full months in advance. If all else fails, you might still get a place on one of eight special daily tours – these are available only as last-minute tickets (€40) and can be purchased the day before from the National Museum of War (Fort St Elmo, Valletta) and the Gozo Museum of Archaeology (Victoria).

section here illustrates how the complex was dug out, first by boring holes using deer antlers, then knocking off chunks of rock between the cavities with stone mallets, and finally polishing and painting the walls. It was in the main chamber of the second level that the iconic "Sleeping Lady" figurine was recovered (see page 33). Further on, the **Oracle Room** is decorated by a painted tree thought to symbolize the tree of life; the room itself takes its name from the Oracle Hole, a

niche which, when spoken into, amplifies voices into echoes that boom through the underground space (similar to the Oracle of Delphi). The purpose of the room known as the Holy of Holies remains a mystery, as no bones were recovered during excavations. In front of its entrance, two linked holes in the ground may have been used to collect libations or solid offerings. The third and youngest level is a complex of smaller spaces reaching 10m underground, which served as mass graves.

RESTAURANTS	
Bongo Nyah	2
Diar il-Bniet	1
Tal Familija	3

Addolorata Cemetery

MAP P.96, POCKET MAP E15
Vjal Santa Lucija, Paola. Daily 7am–4.30pm.
Free. Buses #1–4, #80, #82 and #88 from
Valletta.

Consecrated in 1869, Malta's
largest burial ground, **Addolorata
Cemetery**, is worth exploring for
its Neogothic architecture and
collection of bombastic Baroque-
styled tombs. From the entrance,
a path meanders uphill past
elaborate marble-cased tombstones
(their hotchpotch of designs
is bewildering and beautiful)
overhung by cypress, olives, carobs
and Aleppo pines. At the highest
reaches of the cemetery, the well-to-
do are laid to rest inside sumptuous
mausoleums. The Gothic Revival
chapel at the top of the hill is
closed to the public, but the ornate
exterior is noted for its (rare in
Malta) stained-glass windows.
Addolorata Cemetery also contains
250 Commonwealth burials from

Addolorata Cemetery

Neolithic Malta

Malta's **Neolithic community**, which blossomed from 5000–2500 BCE, was the most advanced civilization of its time. Its temples (almost 25 major sites have been discovered so far) are the oldest freestanding man-made structures in the world and the relics within are more artistically sophisticated than anything found elsewhere of the same period. Yet Neolithic Malta remains shrouded in mystery.

Malta is thought to have supported between 5000 and 10,000 Neolithic inhabitants, and most of that number must have been working on the megalithic temples given the mobilization required to build them – yet the people also had to produce food and build domestic homes. Generations of archaeologists have pored over this contradiction, which is complicated by the fact that in around 2500 BCE the Neolithic community came to an inexplicable and sudden end. The most mainstream explanation is that the inhabitants over-exploited the environment and, with their natural resources dwindling, became obsessed with religious salvation from their predicament. Critics argue that there is no supporting evidence of environmental distress and the erection of the temples is in itself a sign that the people had abundant resources. Another theory holds that Malta was much larger at the time, and what survives is the tip of its mountain, on which most of the temples are concentrated. There is geological plausibility in this: the Pantelleria Rift, southwest of Malta, constantly produces upwarping of the land, and this could have led to a massive earthquake that destroyed the larger part of Malta and its inhabitants. However, there is no hard proof for this or any other theory. The mystery continues.

World War I and eighteen from World War II.

Żejtun

MAP P.96, POCKET MAP F15
Bus #80, #82, #85 and #88 from Valletta.
One of the great pleasures of visiting **Żejtun** is strolling about its quiet sun-dappled streets, soaking up the atmosphere. The town has prospered since Phoenician times, and its name – which means "olive" in Arabic – is evoked today in the annual olive festival, the best time to visit. The village's highlight is **St Catherine's Church**, designed by Lorenzo Gafa in 1692, which dominates the skyline for miles around. The surrounding streets are littered with medieval architectural features, and the most distinctive building, situated near the bus station on Misrah Carlo Diacono, is **Aedes Daniels Palace** with its imposing facade bedecked with large statues. Adjacent are two medieval chapels, and along their southern flank runs Triq Luqa Briffa, which leads east to the town's **old quarter**, where you'll find a maze of twisting alleyways and delightful architectural details.

Marsascala and St Thomas Bay

MAP P.96, POCKET MAP F15
The seaside village of **Marsascala**, well off the tourist track, offers a pleasant taste of everyday life in Malta. Situated on a peninsula that divides two bays, it has evaded the over-development of the central and northern regions.

No surprise, then, that the village has attracted Malta's hippies and artists, who have opened alternative bars and restaurants along Marsascala Bay. A palm-lined promenade snakes from here along the peninsula's perimeter, from which you can see saltpans cut into the shoreline. At the tip of the peninsula stands **St Thomas Tower**, built by Grand Master Alof de Wignacourt in 1614 to protect the southern coast from corsairs. The promenade continues to **St Thomas Bay**, a popular summer swimming spot with good facilities, where chalky white cliffs slope into shallow water.

Sant' Antnin Family Park

MAP P.96, POCKET MAP D15
Triq Sant Antnin, Marsascala. Open 24hr.
Free.

Malta's largest **leisure park**, built in 2013 to rehabilitate a closed landfill, offers a pleasant (and free) diversion for families. The park is home to a picnic area, playgrounds, outdoor gym, rock climbing, dog park, olive grove, football pitch and equestrian area, as well as a petting zoo with goats, llamas, ponies and chickens. Parking is free; bring your own snacks and water.

Ħaġar Qim and Mnajdra Neolithic temples

MAP P.96, POCKET MAP D15
Triq Ħaġar Qim, Qrendi ☎ 2142 4231,
ⓦ heritagemalta.org. Daily 9am–6pm. €10.
Bus #74 from Valletta.

Situated on a rugged and scenic rocky plateau that reaches down to the area's dramatic cliffs, the **Ħaġar Qim** and **Mnajdra Neolithic temple complexes** – constructed between 3600 and 2500 BCE – are Malta's most atmospheric outdoor temples. Sitting less than a kilometre apart, they are a deeply stirring sight – despite the transparent protective shields that were put up in 2008 to protect them from weather erosion.

Visits begin at the excellent visitor centre, which shows a 4D film experience that documents the site's history, from Neolithic construction to discovery in the nineteenth century. Several interactive exhibitions provide a good overview of the possible construction techniques and uses of the temple complexes, with fun

Mnajdra Neolithic temple complex

interpretation material provided for children.

Ħaġar Qim, a circular complex of four temples, where spaces and chambers open into each other in an intricate jumble of rooms, is the least understood of all Maltese temple sites. The understanding of these spaces, and their ceremonial significance, is close to nil. No burial remains have been discovered, although animal sacrifices may have taken place, but most theories do point to a religious purpose: in the rear of one apse, a curious series of low stone slabs form an inner enclosure. On the summer solstice, the sun's rays pass through a small elliptical hole to dramatically illuminate one of the slabs.

A 500m walk along a gently inclining path brings you to the Mnajdra complex, three temples that form a continuous concave facade. At the Central Temple look for the architectural plan carved into one of its megaliths at the time of construction; this is claimed to be the first ever architectural design. The elegant South Temple is the best preserved of any on the Maltese islands. Its main entrance is decorated with small drilled holes to mark the position of the rising sun on the equinoxes and solstices. In its first chamber you'll find the so-called Oracle Hole, a small aperture that opens into a hidden cubicle that's thought to have been the seat of a hidden oracle, who may have passed on messages or interpreted epiphanies during ceremonies. Only the foundations survive of the East Temple.

Wied Iż-Żurrieq and the Blue Grotto

MAP P.96, POCKET MAP E15
Bus #38 or #138 from Valletta. Boats to Blue Grotto daily 9am–5pm (10–20min; €8)

Marsaxlokk

RESTAURANTS
Tartarun — 1
Terrone — 2

ACCOMMODATION
Duncan Guesthouse — 2
Port View Guesthouse — 3
Quayside Apartments — 1

Enclosed by a deep gorge and lying at the mouth of a creek, most people come to the former fishing outpost of **Wied Iż-Żurrieq** to board one of the boats that ferry visitors to the **Blue Grotto** and other smaller caves. The Blue Grotto is a dramatically domed cave opening at sea level, fronted by a buttress eroded into the rocks. The sea within has a deep-blue luminosity, especially in early morning. That said, the wait to get a boat can be hours' long, their drivers aren't particularly affable and the constant boat-traffic ruins the atmosphere.

Filfla

POCKET MAP D16

Filfla is a tiny uninhabited islet located 5km offshore. Its name is believed to come from *felfel*, Arabic for peppercorn. Sadly, until 1971, the British Royal Navy and Air Force used the island for target practice (spent cartridges are still be found today) reducing the island's size and turning its cliffs into mounds of rubble. Since 1980 it has been designated a nature reserve (off limits to the public) in an effort to protect its large colony of storm petrels and its endemic species of wall lizards and door snails.

Marsaxlokk

MAP P.100, POCKET MAP F15
Bus #81 and #75 from Valletta or #TD11 from Sliema and Buġibba.

Marsaxlokk

Marsaxlokk is a must-see on any southern itinerary. Set around the deep scoop of Marsaxlokk Bay, it is home port for Malta's largest fishing fleet, and the spectacle of the town's fishermen and their colourfully painted *luzzu* (wooden boats) remains its principal allure. Marsaxlokk's seafront promenade serves as its town centre, with its church and pedestrianized square set by the shore. At its daily open-air market here hawkers (literally)

Traditional Maltese fishing boats

Demanding great skill to build, traditional *luzzu* are more expensive now than modern fibreglass boats, but most fishermen prefer them for their stability and durability. Fishing here reaches its zenith during the late summer and autumn: the fishing season for lampuki (dolphin fish). Lampuki are uniquely fished using the *kannizzati* method, which has not changed significantly since Roman times. Fishermen cut and gather the large palm fronds and weave them into flat rafts, which are pulled out to sea by *luzzu*. At midday, lampuki schooling under the rafts seeking shade are netted. The eyes painted on the prows of *luzzu* are supposed to lead fishermen to their catch.

St Peter's Pool

sell everything under the sun, including some excellent Maltese lace, local olives, honey, and fresh fish (look for octopus, squid, swordfish, tuna, and sometimes even shark). The most popular day to visit is on Sunday morning when the market is at its biggest and busiest. Most restaurants here cook delectable, fresh seafood (see page 103). Booking ahead is a must, especially on Sundays in the winter when locals descend for long, leisurely seafood lunches.

St Peter's Pool

MAP P.96, POCKET MAP F16
A 30min walk from Marsaxlokk (not advised in the hot summer months).
At scenic **St Peter's Pool** the shore is sculpted by winter storms into a combination of dramatic cliff faces and – the major draw – a crescent-shaped swimming hole cut into the golden limestone. The clear water is an ideal spot for a dip, and some sections of the smooth limestone shores are comfortable for sunbathing. Depending on wind conditions, there can be an issue with unsightly flotsam: it's advisable to visit when the wind is blowing from northern or westerly directions, or when it's dead calm. There are no facilities at St Peter's Pool; bring your own water and snacks.

Għar Dalam Cave and Museum

MAP P.96, POCKET MAP F15
Għar Dalam Road, Birżebbuġa ☎ 2165 7419, ⓦ heritagemalta.org. Daily 9am–5pm. €5. Bus #80 and #82 from Valletta.
Although billed as a major sight, **Għar Dalam Cave and Museum** is of minor appeal. The cave is considered the place where Malta's human story began, so the site should be fascinating, but the dusty Victorian-style exhibits here are mostly limited to bones. Excavations of the 145m-deep cave (only 50m of which are accessible to visitors), mostly carried out following its discovery in 1892, yielded human teeth and a skull that were dated to 7000 years ago, making them Malta's earliest human remains. Other finds include the remains of prehistoric animals, such as hippopotamus and dwarf elephants, flushed into the cave at the end of the last Ice Age, when the level of the Mediterranean was considerably lower than it is today and Malta was connected to Europe via land bridges.

Pretty Bay

MAP P.96
Bus #X4 from Valletta.
As its name suggests, **Pretty Bay** is easy on the eye, boasting Malta's most tropical-looking beach, with soft white sand and turquoise waters. The only catch is that it overlooks Malta's massive Freeport – the twelfth busiest in Europe. To put a positive spin on things, it can be fascinating to lie back on the beach and watch the massive tankers unload – the contrast is memorable.

Restaurants

Bongo Nyah

MAP P.96

3 Triq il-Gardiel, Marsaskala ☎ 9985 5057,
Ⓦ bongonyah.com.mt. Tues–Fri 6pm–1am,
Sat–Sun noon–1am.

A family-friendly restaurant
popular with Malta's artsy set.
Food options run from healthy
salads (€10–13) to burgers (€13),
washed down with local draught
craft beer (€4). Frequent live music
sessions. Mains €10–23.

Diar il-Bniet

MAP P.96

Triq il-Kbira, Dingli ☎ 2762 0727,
Ⓦ diarilbniet.com. Mon–Sat 11am–11pm,
Sun 10am–8pm.

Alongside *Tal-Petut* in Birgu (see
page 53), *Diar il-Bniet* offers
the best taste of Maltese rural
food on the island. Everything
here, down to the cheese and
olive oil, is handmade with
ingredients grown on the
restaurant's 600-acre farm.
The menu changes seasonally,
and typically includes rustic
farmhouse pies (€10), gourds
stuffed with spiced minced beef
(€14), and deliciously sweet-and-
sour aubergine *kapunata* (€7).

Tal Familija

MAP P.96

Triq il-Gardiel, Marsascala ☎ 2163 2161,

Ⓦ talfamiljarestaurant.com. Tues–Sun
noon–10.30pm.

An airy restaurant spread across
three intimate dining areas,
specializing in homely Maltese
cooking with an emphasis on fresh
fish and shellfish (€17–22) and
typical Italian pastas (€10).

Tartarun

MAP P.100

29 Xatt is-Sajjieda, Marsaxlokk ☎ 2165
8089, Ⓦ tartarun.com. Tues–Sat noon–
3.30pm & 7.30–10.30pm, Sun noon–3.30pm.

Fresh line-caught fish are the star of
the show at *Tartarun*, where chefs
put creative twists on traditional
recipes using seasonal ingredients.
Think black tortellini with local
prawns and crabs in a fermented
honey veloute (€13) or langoustine
(€10/100g) served with preserved-
citrus couscous.

Terrone

MAP P.100

1 Triq il-Wilga, Marsaxlokk ☎ 2704 2656,
Ⓦ terrone.com.mt. Mon–Fri noon–11pm,
Sat 8am–11pm, Sun 8am–10pm.

Located across from Marsasxlokk's
seafront promenade, the menu
at *Terrone* changes almost daily
according to what's fresh. Dishes
include smoky chargrilled calamari
(€18), *strozzapreti* pasta with fresh
yellowfin tuna and pine nuts (€14),
and dreamy pistachio and honey
cake with pistachio gelato (€7) – all
sure bets.

Bongo Nyah

Gozo

Gozo offers a delightful mix of historic attractions and rural tranquillity, with a dramatic coastline dominated by headlands and large bays in the north, and a girdle of cliffs interspersed with gorges in the south. The slow and easy pace of life here is irresistible, while the island is increasingly on the radar of outdoor-sports enthusiasts, offering superb scuba diving, rock climbing, canoeing and hiking. Gozo may not seem all that different from its sister island, but spend a little time here and the contrasts become apparent: sleepier villages clustered around deep, verdant valleys of handsome terraced hills; and low-slung townscapes that blessedly lack Malta's high-rises.

Entertainment mostly revolves around cafés by day and restaurants in the evening, the latter serving hearty Gozitan dishes alongside Italian classics. There are only a dozen or so hotels, concentrated in the seaside towns of Marsalforn and Xlendi.

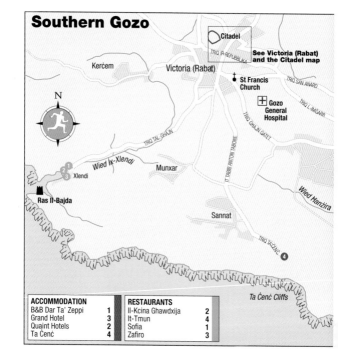

Southern Gozo

Citadel

TRIQ IR-REPUBBLIKA

See Victoria (Rabat) and the Citadel map

Kerċem

Victoria (Rabat)

St Francis Church

TRIQ SAN ANARD

Gozo General Hospital

TRIQ L-IMGARR

N

TRIQ TAL-GHAJN

TRIQ GHAJN QATET

IT-TABRI ANTON TABONE

Wied Ix-Xlendi

Munxar

Xlendi

Ras Il-Bajda

Wied Hanzira

Sannat

TRIQ TA'ĊENĊ

Ta Ċenċ Cliffs

ACCOMMODATION		RESTAURANTS	
B&B Dar Ta' Zeppi	1	Il-Kcina Ghawdxija	2
Grand Hotel	3	It-Tmun	4
Quaint Hotels	2	Sofia	1
Ta Ċenċ	4	Zafiro	3

Most people stay in luxuriously converted farmhouses or B&Bs in smaller villages across the island. The Gozitans themselves are affable, close-knit, deeply religious and justifiably proud of their little island. Although locals are outnumbered year-round by tourists, they are renowned for their warm hospitality.

Victoria

MAP P.106, POCKET MAP B11

Gozo's pleasant capital, **Victoria** (in Maltese, Rabat, though easily confused with Malta's own village of Rabat), is dominated by the *Ċittadella* and defined by its main thoroughfare, Triq ir-Repubblika (Republic Street), which cuts across the town. Here you'll find the island's largest concentration of shops, Gozo's main theatres (the Astra and Aurora) and the Villa Rundle Gardens, a little haven of shade in the summer heat and the stage for outdoor concerts during summer months. However, it's the old part of town that holds the most charm, its maze of alleys lined with pretty townhouses, elaborately carved stone balconies and niches containing Catholic icons. The area is quiet and pedestrianised, bounded at the north by Pjazza l-Indipendenza, a tree lined square laid out in front of the Banca Giuratale, an unusual circular Baroque building from 1733 that is now the town hall. The morning tourist market in this square offers kitsch souvenirs, but the cafés (see page 120) surrounding it have outdoor tables that are great for soaking up the scene. The square adjoins Pjazza San Ġorġ to the south, dominated by the ornate **St George's Basilica** (daily 7am–noon & 2.30–7.30pm; free), the most sumptuously Baroque of Gozo's churches.

SHOP
Vini e Capricci 1

BAR
Gleneagles 1

Xaghra
Ġgantija Temples

Ramla Valley

TRIQ IR-RABAT

TRIQ IT-TIGRIJA

TRIQ L-QALA

Nadur

TRIQ XAGHRA

❶

Xewkija ❷

St John the Baptist

TRIQ L-IMGARR

TRIQ SANT'ANTNIN

Ghajnsielem

Mġarr ❸
❹

Mġarr Harbour

TRIQ L-IMGARR

Mġarr Ix-Xini

| 0 | | mile | | 1 |
| 0 | kilometre | | 1 | |

The Ċittadella

MAP P.106, POCKET MAP B11

Visitor centre daily 9.30am–5pm; free

Gozo's recently restored bulwark **castle**, commanding a ridge overlooking Victoria, is the island's oldest settlement and shortlisted to become a UNESCO World Heritage Site. The visitor centre, housed in a nineteenth-century water cistern at the base of the citadel, is unmissable, offering an excellent 360-degree documentary film experience.

The Ċittadella, which traces its beginnings to 2500 BCE, was under the control of various occupying forces until a City Council was established in the fourteenth century. By the time the Knights arrived in 1530, over five thousand people were living in the Ċittadella. In 1551 nearly all of them were dragged into slavery when Ottoman corsair Dragut Rias laid siege. After this disaster,

the City Council put forth a contentious regulation requiring all remaining Gozitans on the island to sleep in the Ċittadella between May and October, when the calm seas were rife with corsairs. The regulation was not repealed until 1637.

The main attraction of the Ċittadella is **Gozo Cathedral** (daily 5am–8pm), which was designed by the celebrated Maltese architect Lorenzo Gafa and built between 1697 and 1711. Funds ran out before the cathedral's dome was built, so the interior of the "flat dome" now features a spectacular *trompe l'oeil* painting of a false dome. The **Cathedral Museum** at the back of the church (separate entrance on Triq Fosos) holds a disorienting jumble of the church's historic artefacts; if you're pressed for time, it's easily skipped.

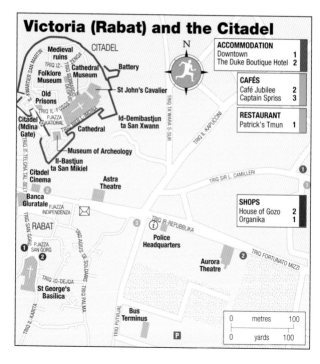

Victoria (Rabat) and the Citadel

ACCOMMODATION
Downtown   1
The Duke Boutique Hotel   2

CAFÉS
Café Jubilee   2
Captain Spriss   3

RESTAURANT
Patrick's Tmun   1

SHOPS
House of Gozo   2
Organika   1

Visiting Gozo

The main link between the islands is provided by 24hr **ferries** (☎ 2210 9000, Ⓦ gozochannel.com; every 45min in daytime, every 2hr at night; 25min) between Ċirkewwa in Malta and Mġarr Harbour in Gozo. Foot-passenger tickets cost €4.65; it's €15.70 for a car and one driver. Gozo's main **bus** station is on Triq Putirjal in Rabat, with buses calling at most of Gozo's towns from 5.30am to 11pm. You can get a bus schedule from the tourist office on Triq Ir-Repubblika in Victoria, or at Ⓦ publictransport.com.mt. You can pick up **taxis** at the Mġarr ferry terminal or at Victoria's bus terminal and Independence Square. White taxis (equipped with meters) can be hailed. For private cars and airport transfers try Mayjo Car Rentals (☎ 2155 6678, Ⓦ mayjocarhire.com; Malta International Airport to Gozo from €65). Double-decker hop-on hop-off **tour buses** cover all major tourist sites (10am–7pm; day tickets from €20). Street **parking** around Gozo is free and ample (look for spaces marked in white). Rabat also has two large free car parks located several blocks apart on Triq Giorgio Borg Oliver. Next to the main entrance of the Citadel there is also a small private paid car park (€1.75).

The other focus points of a visit to the Ċittadella are its four **museums**, only two of which are worth checking out (Ⓦ heritage malta.org; all daily 9am–5pm; €3 each, €8 for all four, €13 for a combined ticket for all Heritage Malta Gozo sites/museums).

The first of these is the **Archaeology Museum**, a small repository of relics discovered in Gozo, spanning all periods from the Neolithic to the Arabic era and detailing the discovery of the Ġgantija temples and the priceless ancient artefacts found within. Top exhibits include the fascinating and voluptuous Neolithic stone figurines that would be at home in any contemporary art museum, amulets representing Egyptian deities found in the limits of Xewkija and, from the Arabic epoch, a marvelous marble tombstone with a long and poetic dedication.

Gozo was used as a place of exile since antiquity, when Byzantine emperor Heraclius (610–641 BCE) sent his conspiring son Theodorus to die here. The sixteenth-century **Old Prison** is Gozo's last site of exile and the Ċittadella's other notable museum. The most famous inmate here was Jean de la Valette

Cathedral of the Assumption

Folklore Museum

(the Grand Master at the time of the Great Siege, for whom Valletta was named), who was imprisoned for four months for attacking a layman. Today, the prison cell walls bear the graffiti left by former inmates, which was discovered when a layer of lime whitewash was removed during rehabilitation works. Frequent motifs include the outline of a palm (akin to a signature), galleys, calendars and even games.

The **Folklore Museum** holds mildly diverting implements of traditional trades, the largest of which is a mule-driven wheat mill. The building itself, a medieval Siculo-Norman house that's full of nooks and crannies, is more interesting than its contents. The fourth and final museum, the **Natural History Museum**, is of marginal interest, with panels illustrating Gozo's geology, as well as some ad-hoc displays dedicated to flora and fauna,

ACCOMMODATION	
Ellie Boo Bed & Breakfast	2
Gozo Escape	3
Maria Giovanna Guest House	4
Murella Living B&B	1

RESTAURANTS	
Murella	1
Ta Frenċ	2

SHOP	
Charlie's Antiques	1

including a depressed flock of dusty, stuffed birds.

Visiting the Citadel's museums is not essential to appreciating this ancient site, but wandering the length of its **ramparts** absolutely is. A stroll is enriched by the free Ċittadella app (visitgozo.com), which provides a custom audio tour based on your location within the fortress.

Xewkija

MAP P.104, POCKET MAP B11–12
Bus #323 and #301 from Victoria.

The main reason to visit **Xewkija** – one of the oldest villages in Gozo – is to see the massive **St John the Baptist Church** on Pjazza San Ġwann Battista (daily 6am–noon & 4–7pm; free), whose dome is visible from all over Gozo. The Baroque design is by the Italian Giuseppe Damato, inspired by the Basilica of Santa Maria Della Salute in Venice. Its dimensions

are impressive: supported by eight internal pillars, the honey-coloured 75m-high dome is the tallest in Gozo, while the building's internal volume is only slightly smaller than St Peter's Cathedral in Rome. It's an awe-inspiring structure, built over a forty-year period with the donated funds of the faithful and the donated time of local skilled craftsmen.

Mġarr Ix-Xini

MAP P.104
Bus #301 from Victoria.

The signposted road from Xewkija to **Mġarr Ix-Xini** (which is rough but safely passable) meanders past cattle farms along the south flank of the dramatic **Ħanżira Valley**, a gorge cut into the bedrock by an ancient river – now a popular spot for rock-climbing. The valley meets the sea at Mġarr Ix-Xini, a tranquil fjord fronted by a small patch of pebbly shore, where the transparent water beckons you for

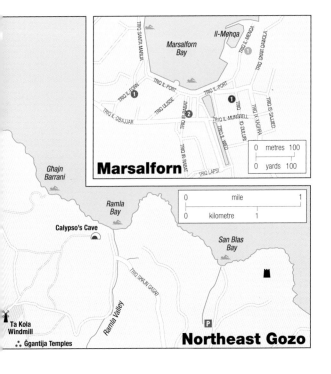

a dip. Mġarr Ix-Xini translates as "the harbour of the galleys", referring to the time when it provided a hidden anchorage for corsairs' frequent raids on Gozo. Nowadays, its beauty attracts yachts to drop anchor but, absent from the usual boat tour circuit, the bay is a relatively hidden gem (for now, at least). At the mouth of Mġarr Ix-Xini lies the largest **coastal watchtower** erected in Gozo, whose construction by the Knights in 1658 effectively deterred the activities of marauders. An old cobbled path leads from the bay to the tower, which is operated by heritage NGO Wirt Ghawdex and is open to the public on Saturdays (Sat 11am–1.30pm or whenever the flag is flying; free).

Ta Ċenċ Cliffs

MAP P.104, POCKET MAP B12
Bus #305 from Victoria.

Just outside the nondescript town of Sannat, the land falls sharply into the sea at **Ta Ċenċ**. With sweeping views of the sea stretching towards the horizon, it's a very scenic spot for a walk (there are no picnic facilities or bathrooms, so

Xlendi

take your own water); the rocky *garigue* (a rugged habitat of hardy bushes) supports some interesting local fauna and flora. Clumps of rock centaury – Malta's national plant, with small, succulent leaves and fluffy mauve flowers in summer – cling to the cliff edge, and the area is a favoured haunt of the blue rock thrush, the national bird, easily identifiable by its dark brown or blue plumage and habit of flicking its tail feathers up and down. Ta Ċenċ is best known, however, for its one thousand or so pairs of Cory's shearwaters that nest in crags on the cliff face when they're not spending the day at sea. As one of the largest colonies in the Mediterranean, they make this an Important Bird Area (IBA) according to BirdLife International.

Xlendi

MAP P.104, POCKET MAP A11–12
Bus #306 from Victoria.

Xlendi, a picturesque seaside village, is an essential stop on any Gozo itinerary. Top billing goes to the compact waterfront, which fronts a pebbly beach lined with cafés and restaurants, and is popular for long, leisurely lunches – especially on Sundays when extended Maltese families catch up over heaving plates of food. Xlendi is a designated swimming zone during the summer, and also offers excellent snorkelling and diving. Canoes and paddleboats, a great way to explore the bay's many caves, are available to rent at the small wharf (€5). From the wharf, a white staircase ascends the great limestone hill that long made Xlendi bay a favourite refuge for ships since Roman times (a large number of amphora have been found on the seabed in the mouth of the bay). Head up and over the hill to reach Caroline's Cave, formerly the property of a wealthy woman from Victoria who donated it to the local Augustinian nuns so they could enjoy their very own secluded swimming hole. Continue west along Xlendi's promenade for delightful views of the sheer cliffs on Gozo's southern coast, which until a few generations ago were favoured by the area's so-called "climbing fishermen", who inched down to ledges near the bottom to fish in the deep waters. This path, built by the Knights, leads to the coastal Xlendi Tower at the mouth of the bay, built by Grand Master Juan de Lascaris-Castellar in 1650 as a defence against corsairs.

Marsalforn

MAP P.108, POCKET MAP B11
Bus #310 from Victoria.

On the opposite northern coast from Xlendi, **Marsalforn** is Gozo's largest seaside resort, consisting of a ribbon of inexpensive apartment blocks and small hotels spread across a large bay, particularly popular with British tourists and retirees. Despite its mass of buildings, the bay has an open feel and for much of the year it feels like a resort in low season – only on summer evenings does a bustle of strollers build and the seafront restaurants fill up. There's some

Xwejni saltpans

traditional colour at Il-Menqa, a small breakwater-enclosed harbour on the east flank of the bay that's the docking station for a dwindling number of brightly painted *luzzi* fishing boats; otherwise, there isn't much else to distract you from lounging by the sea. During the summer, you can swim at a small sandy beach at the inner mouth of the bay; most locals prefer to swim off the rocks that trace the waterline along the west side of the bay, where the promenade gives way to the rocky shoreline (there are ladders for getting in and out).

Xwejni saltpans

MAP P.108
Bus #310 from Victoria.

Gozo's **saltpans** – a web of geometric depressions gouged into the soft yellow globigerina limestone – take up a 2km by 50m strip of the island's coastline. During winter, heavy waves splatter seawater over the rocks to fill the pans; this evaporates during the summer, leaving thick crusts of crystal salt. If you visit in August, you'll see gangs of workers shovelling the salt into bags; the uncrushed crystals

Xagħra

are sold in most local supermarkets. The pans are beautiful, particularly during winter, when the reflection of the sky in the water-filled pans makes it look like a field of mirrors.

Wied Il-Għasri

MAP P.108, POCKET MAP A11
Bus #309 from Victoria.

A deep, snaking gorge some 300m long with a creek at the bottom, **Wied Il-Għasri** (Għasri Valley) is reached via the right fork of the road beyond the last saltpans, or from the village of Żabbar via a short hike down Triq is-Saghtrija. A flight of stairs pickaxed into the side of the cliff leads to the inner mouth of the creek and a tiny pebbly shore. This is an excellent spot for diving and snorkelling in the summer; look out for rays, deep-water fish and some curious underwater topography towards the outer reaches of the creek.

Xagħra

MAP P.104, POCKET MAP B11
Bus #307 from Victoria.

One of Gozo's largest towns, **Xagħra** sprawls over a series of ridges and bluffs. It's a comparatively busy place, with an attractive and lively town square, Pjazza Vittorja (Victory Square), fringed by oleander trees and handsome Baroque townhouses abutted by old colonial-era bars. At the head of the square stands the Church of the Nativity of Our Lady, a fine example of an eighteenth-century village church, with its ornate bell towers, dome, and an overwhelmingly gold-and-crimson interior.

Ġgantija temples

MAP P.104, POCKET MAP B11
Triq John Otto Bayer, Xagħra ☎ 2155 3194, Ⓦ heritagemalta.org. Daily 9am–5pm. €6 or €9 combined with Ta Kola Windmill. Bus #307 from Victoria.

Of all the Neolithic temples in the Maltese islands, the two at **Ġgantija** are perhaps the most evocative and impressive; they're also the oldest freestanding man-made structures in the world, erected around 3600 BCE and predating Stonehenge and the Egyptian pyramids. The word Ġgantija derives from the word Ġgant (giant), since the Gozitans used to believe the temples were built by a race of giants – when you see the size of the limestone blocks here, you might well agree. This complex of temples laid under an accumulation of rubble for thousands of years before being discovered and excavated in 1827. Since then, erosion has taken a heavy toll, but the half-ruined edifice remains an imposing sight with its megalithic walls projecting over the bluff it's situated on – the largest megalith, weighing 55 tonnes, is as big as a lorry. The circular complex comprises two temples, and their form and layout, as well as the artefacts found within them, suggest they were an important ritual focus of a highly organised society. Remains of animal bone and stone hearths point to rituals involving animal sacrifices. A number of libation holes in the floor may have been used for the pouring of liquid offerings, and decorated features found inside the temples include patterns of drilled holes and bas-relief panels depicting spiral motifs, trees, plants and various animals. The complex is accessed through a new Interpretation Centre, built to accommodate the 200,000 tourists who visit the site every year. It's worth lingering here to learn more about daily life in the Neolithic period and the theories on how the temples were constructed and used, besides viewing a fascinating selection of prehistoric artefacts found on Gozo.

Ta Kola Windmill

MAP P.108
Triq Il-Mithna, Xaghra ☎ 2156 1071, ⊛ heritagemalta.org. Daily 9am–5pm. €2.30. Buses #64 and #65 from Victoria.
The oldest surviving **windmill** built by the Knights is now open as a tourist attraction, having ceased commercial wheat-grinding at the beginning of the twentieth century. When the wind was right for the mill to operate, the miller would blow through a triton-shell

(in Maltese, *bronja*) to let villagers know to bring their grain to be ground into flour. The original, intact apparatus that turned the grinding stones is still in situ: a complex series of huge cogwheels fashioned entirely out of timber. On the upper floor, the millers' re-created living quarters offer a view on daily rural life in Gozo, including a kitchen decked out with a traditional *kenur*, a stone hearth used for stewing.

Calypso's Cave

MAP P.108, POCKET MAP B11
Bus #302 from Victoria. On foot, take the path from Ramla Bay beach. By car, go via the village of Xagħra; you've arrived when you reach a small car park and gift shop.
Perched on a bluff above the sea, **Calypso's Cave** is (misleadingly) touted as the legendary grotto inhabited by the nymph Calypso in Homer's *Odyssey*, where she kept Odysseus captive through love for seven years. In Homer's work, that grotto was on an island called Ogygia and, although evidence exists that Gozo was once called Ogygia, the proof that

Calypso's Cave

this is the true Calypso's Cave is circumstantial (muddling things further, some researchers also claim that the real cave is situated in a valley in Mellieħa). The unimpressive cave itself, formed by fissures in the rock surface, is closed to the public due to unstable geological movement. However, a viewing platform offers a gorgeous scene of clay slopes tumbling down to the orange sand of Ramla Bay and rolling inland into Ramla Valley – you can pick out the town of Nadur on a ledge at the valley's far side.

Ramla Bay

MAP P.108, POCKET MAP B11
Bus #302 from Victoria.

Enclosed by twin headlands, little **Ramla Bay** is among the most stunning beaches in the Mediterranean. Set at the mouth of a large valley and flanked by high ridges, the beach is a strip

of soft, bright-orange-coloured sand that gives way to a sweep of clear shallow sea. At the back of the beach, the sand rises into dunes that are bound by tamarisk trees – the only sand-dune habitat in the Maltese islands, and home to rare plants and insects (avoid lying or walking here). The bay also holds two historical attractions: an underground wall built by the Knights to hinder enemy boats from landing and, on the eastern flank of the bay, a *fougasse* – a rock-cut mortar that was designed to be filled with rocks and gunpowder and fired on enemy vessels attempting to break through the underwater wall. Ramla is attractive at any time of the year – it's a great spot for a stroll in winter, and the best beach in Gozo for swimming in the summer – but it gets understandably crowded in July and August, especially on

Western Gozo

ACCOMMODATION
Kempinski San
Lawrenz Resort 1

SHOP
Ta Dbieġi Crafts Village 1

RESTAURANT
Gazebo 1

San Dimitri Chapel

Ta Ġordan Lighthouse

Ta Ġordan Hill

Church of the Visitation

Folklore Museum

Ta' Pinu Basilica

Gharb

TRIQ IL-KNISJA

Ta Ġjammar Hill

The remains of the Azure Window

Inland Sea

San Lawrenz

TRIQ FRANĠISK PORTELLI

TRIQ IL-GĦARB

DWEJRA

TRIQ IR-ROKON

Dwejra Tower

Wied il-Mielaħ

Fungus Rock (Il-Ġebla Tal-General)

Dwejra Bay

N

0 ____ mile ____ 1
0 ____ kilometre ____ 1

Ramla Bay

Sundays. For a quieter spot, there's a small sandy creek on the western flank of the bay, reached via a ten-minute walk from the beach proper along a path that skirts the shoreline. Parking is on the wide access road and private fields that are turned into a temporary car park in the summer; just before the beach, a couple of operators rent umbrellas and sun loungers (€8/day). Kiosks serve drinks and snacks, and old-school ice-cream trucks occasionally drop by. There are also public toilet and shower facilities available.

San Blas Bay

MAP P.108, POCKET MAP C11
Buses #302 and 303 from Victoria.
San Blas, a small, sandy beach with red-orange sand, is like a miniature version of Ramla. It has been left in its pristine natural state, and the only commercial activity is a portable kiosk where you can rent umbrellas and sun loungers (€10 for two), or have a drink and snack (mostly chips and burgers, but sometimes fresh prawn and calamari if you're lucky). It's a scenic spot for a day by the sea, snorkelling in its shallow water or sunbathing. The downside of San Blas's natural glory is limited access: unless you're driving, you have to walk for half an hour from Nadur's town centre. Even if you're driving, the farmers' access road is a narrow concrete strip that is closed to traffic from halfway down because it is exceptionally steep. During high season, privately owned Jeeps offer rides up and down the hill for €3 per person (you can negotiate better rates for a group). Portable toilets are offered during the summer months, but expect fewer facilities in the winter.

Ta' Pinu Basilica

MAP P.114, POCKET MAP A11
☏ 2155 6187. Daily 6.30am–noon & 3.30–7pm. Free. Bus #308 from Victoria.
A couple of kilometres west of Rabat lies the imposing **Ta' Pinu Basilica**, Gozo's primary pilgrimage site. The church had its beginnings as a medieval chapel, but by 1575 had fallen into disrepair and was marked for demolition. However, the worker who struck the first sledgehammer

Ta' Pinu Basilica

blow apparently broke his arm – an incident interpreted as a divine sign, which led to the chapel being spared. In 1883, legend has it that Ta' Pinu gained more notoriety when a local fieldworker, Karmela Grima, heard a disembodied voice summoning her to the chapel to "recite three Hail Marys in honour of the three days my body was confined to the tomb." Grima's story spread like wildfire, and islanders began following the voice's call. The present church was built between 1920 and 1932 to accommodate the ever-increasing number of pilgrims who still visit today. The handsome church itself is set in the midst of open countryside overlooking a terraced green valley. Its limestone interior is packed with ornate stone sculptures, but most interesting is the original medieval chapel itself at the back of the present church. The corridors on either side of the altar that lead to the chapel are cluttered floor to ceiling with votive offerings (crutches, braces, shoes, framed photographs, and letters of devotion from around the world) left by those allegedly healed by the church's miracles. Opposite the church, the Stations of the Cross have been reproduced with life-size marble statues lining a route up the Ta Ghammar hill – a popular pilgrimage route, especially during Easter. The view from the top of the hill, which takes in northwest Gozo's motley sweep of fields and compact towns, is worth the walk.

Għarb

MAP P.114, POCKET MAP A11
Bus #312 from Victoria.

Għarb is the most traditional village in Gozo. It's also the sleepiest. Until recently, it was populated almost exclusively by people who worked the surrounding fields and retained an old Maltese dialect, with a vocabulary of words and pronunciations long since discarded by the rest of the population. Lately, it has attracted second-home buyers and many of its buildings are now converted into luxuriously

Fungus Rock

Fungus Rock became renowned in the eighteenth century following the discovery of a parasitic plant that was thought to have medicinal and mythological powers. By 1746, the Knights had put the rock under 24-hour guard to preserve the plant for the privileged use of European rulers. Science eventually discounted the alleged medicinal properties, but the rock remains out of bounds to protect the tuber's only habitat in Malta. Phallus-shaped and covered in tiny, velvety brownish-red flowers, the plant's resemblance to a mushroom earned it the (incorrect) common of "Malta Fungus." It grows abundantly here, but is relatively rare elsewhere in the world.

rustic villas. The swimming pools and landscaped gardens haven't detracted from Gharb's appeal, though, with its pretty streets and expansive vistas. The village's **Church of the Visitation**, located in Pjazza taż-Żjara, was completed in 1732 and boasts an unusual and striking concave façade. Take a short walk outside of the village towards the coastal cliffs to visit the tiny, charming chapel of St Demetrius. A longer hike on the road along Wied il-Mielah brings you through the fertile Gozitan countryside (a sea of yellow Cape Sorrel flowers in the spring) to the sea, where you can find **il-Mielah Window**, Gozo's "other Azure window" – all the more appealing since its big sister disappeared during a storm in 2017. The sea below, only accessible by boat, is an outstanding dive site. With Gharb village known for its skilled craftsmen and lace makers, it's worth checking out the nearby Ta' Dbieġi Crafts Village (see page 119).

Dwejra

Mekren's Bakery

Dwejra

MAP P.114
Bus #311 from Victoria.

Dwejra is most famous for what is no longer there. The iconic **Azure Window**, a picturesque natural opening in the cliffs some 100m in height and width, was lost to rough seas during an intense winter storm in 2017. The window was created by wave erosion over the centuries – a process that had significantly accelerated in recent years – and ultimately destroyed by the same forces. The loss of the Azure Window was deeply mourned by Gozitans and anyone who was lucky enough to see it in person. However, Dwejra still has plenty to recommend it, with distorted, crater-like topography that makes for some very scenic walking. Offshore, the underwater cliffs, valleys, massive plateaux, coral-supporting caves and – nowadays – the remains of the Azure Window offer excellent scuba diving (see page 144).

The bus from Victoria drops you at a car park near the **Inland Sea**, a landlocked body of seawater connected to the Mediterranean via a tunnel in the towering cliff face. In the opposite direction, southeast of the car park, another path takes you to **Dwejra Tower**, part of the coastal defence chain built by the Knights. Beyond the tower is the horseshoe-shaped **Dwejra Bay**, at whose mouth **Fungus Rock** (*Il-Ġebla Tal-General*) – the result of a partial seabed collapse over 23 million years ago – soars 70m out of the sea into a stout pinnacle.

Gozitan ftiras

Traditional Gozitan pizzas (called *ftiras*, but not to be confused with the Maltese bread of the same name) are still made by two bakeries in Nadur town. Traditionally, *ftiras* came in two forms – either topped with anchovies, tomatoes, onions and potatoes or as closed pizzas stuffed with sheep's cheese beaten into eggs – but now most bakeries have introduced other varieties. Best of Nadur's two bakeries is Maxokk Bakery (21 Triq San Ġakbu, ☎ 2155 0014; Mon–Sat 10.30am–7pm, Sun 1–7pm), where the bready *ftiras* (€6–7) are cooked in a wood-fired oven. If you prefer a dough that's easier on your teeth, go to Mekren's Bakery (Triq Ħanaq, ☎ 2155 2342; daily 9am–7pm), which does larger *ftiras* (€5–6) with a crumblier dough. If you're not able to get to Nadur, try the less authentic but passable *ftira* (€9) at Kċina Għawdxija in Xlendi, with its pie-like crust.

Shops

Charlie's Antiques

MAP P.108

Triq id-Duluri, Marsalforn. Tues–Sat noon–6pm

Offers a delightfully odd assortment of vintage bric-a-brac and World War II paraphernalia, including shell casings, Victorian prams, traditional wooden Gozitan lace bobbins, and heaps of funky film cameras. Unlike most thrift shops, *Charlie's* is meticulously organised, making it easy to find one-of-a-kind souvenirs.

House of Gozo

MAP P.106

1 Pjazza San Ġorġ, Victoria ☏ 7930 5688. Mon–Sat 10am–7pm.

A modern souvenir shop selling beautiful souvenir art prints, handmade greeting cards and postcards of Gozitan landmarks.

Organika

MAP P.106

13 Pjazza San Ġorġ, Victoria ☏ 2701 5548, Ⓦ organika.com.mt.

An eclectic shop where the focus is on fairtrade and organic products (primarily jewellery, clothing, art pieces, chocolates and teas) ethically sourced from around the world, as well as affordable souvenirs such as local sea salt.

Ta Dbieġi Crafts Village

MAP P.114

Triq Franġisk Portelli, San Lawrenz ☏ 2155 3977, Ⓦ gozoartisans.com. Daily 10am–5pm.

A cluster of artisan workshops producing and selling good-quality and relatively inexpensive local crafts such as ceramics, leather goods, Maltese lace, wool sweaters and filigree jewellery.

Vini e Capricci

MAP P.104

Gozitano Agricultural Village, Triq l-Imġarr, Xewkija ☏ 2156 3231, Ⓦ viniecapricci.com. Mon–Sat 8am–6pm.

A superb selection of fine Italian charcuterie, a large wine cellar, and several Gozitan artisan food brands make this an ideal place to load up on delicious souvenirs.

Ta Dbieġi Crafts Village

Cafés

Café Jubilee

MAP P.106

Pjazza l-Indipendenza, Victoria ☎ 2155
8921. Mon–Thurs 8am–noon, Fri & Sat
8am–2am.

This café-bar attracts regulars for
its coffee and daytime snacks,
becoming more of a quiet bar with
good music in the evenings. You
can't go wrong with a local lager
and *pastizzi* (€0.75) – their *pastizzi*
are the best on the island – or the
superb rustic ravioli (€9) for lunch.

Captain Spriss

MAP P.106

66 Main Gate St, Victoria ☎ 2156 9112.
Daily 8am–7pm.

A charming Italian café on
Victoria's busiest street that is
excellent for breakfast, with fresh
croissants (€1.20) and proper
Italian coffee.

Restaurants

Gazebo

MAP P.114

Triq ir-Rokon, Kempinski Hotel. ☎ 2211
0000, ⓦ kempinski.com. May–Sept daily
12.30–3.30pm & 7–10.30pm

Café Jubilee

Located in the lush gardens of the
Kempinski Hotel, the romantic
Gazebo restaurant is only open
during the summer and serves a
superb selection of local seafood
enhanced with locally foraged herbs
such as sea asparagus from Dwejra.
For turf rather than surf, try the
homemade violet potato gnocchi
with asparagus, pine nuts and
pecorino (€14). The minted melon
with orange blossom ice cream and
lime fizz dessert (€6) is as delicious
as it is fun.

Il-Kcina Ghawdxija

MAP P.104

Xatt ix-Xlendi, Xlendi ☎ 2156 9118,
ⓦ ilkcinaghawdxija.com. Daily
10.30am–11.30pm.

You'll pay more to experience
traditional Gozitan fare here than
in a typical village restaurant, but
the view of Xlendi Bay is worth it.
Try the Gozitan rabbit stew (€16),
grilled pork chops served with eggs
(€16) or a ftira, akin to a pizza,
filled with beaten eggs, fresh local
cheese and potatoes (€9).

It-Tmun

MAP P.104

Triq Martino Garces, Mġarr ☎ 2156 6276,
ⓦ tmunmgarr.com. Mon–Thurs & Sat
noon–2pm & 6.30–10pm, Wed 6.30–10pm,
Sun noon–2pm.

In operation for over 25 years,
Tmun has established an excellent
reputation with locals for its
upscale but hearty cuisine served
in an elegant, nautically themed
atmosphere. The *bouillabaisse* with
calamari, prawns and shellfish
(€20 for two), and whole fresh fish
al sale (baked in salt) are house
specialities.

Murella

MAP P.108

Triq il-Menqa, Marsalforn ☎ 2156 2473.
Mon–Fri 11am–3pm & 6–11pm, Sat & Sun
10am–11pm.

A relaxed family restaurant set on
the seafront in Marsalforn serving
pasta, wood-fired pizza, grills and

salads. For a taste of local flavours, try the Gozitan *ftira* (see page 118). Mains €9–25.

Patrick's Tmun

MAP P.106

Triq l-Ewropa, Victoria ☏ 2156 6667, ⓦ patrickstmun.com. Mon–Sat 6.30–10.30pm, Sun (winter only) noon–2.30pm.

Located in an unassuming townhouse in Victoria, the atmosphere at *Patrick's Tmun* is like its cuisine – elegant and comforting. Go à la carte or try a tasting menu, with daily specials that emphasize seasonal ingredients. The traditional Gozitan fish soup, *aljotta* (€8), is delicious, while the chargrilled steaks (€23–33) are what *Patrick's* flawless reputation is built on. The extensive wine list is recognized as the best in the country, and includes many rare vintages.

Sofia

MAP P.104

Triq ix-Xlendi, Xlendi ☏ 9971 2623. Mon–Sat 6–11pm, Sun 12.30–3pm & 6–11pm.

A charming taverna set apart from the busy promenade at the bottom of Xlendi valley, *Sofia* is a Greek and Balkan restaurant that prides itself on having no pizza or pasta on its menu (a rarity in Gozo!). Mix and match grilled kebabs to create your own sharing platter (€8–16 each) and wash them down with Bulgarian wine.

Ta Frenċ

MAP P.108

Triq Għajn Damma, Victoria ☏ 2155 3888, ⓦ tafrencrestaurant.com. Mon & Wed–Sun noon–1.30pm & 7–9.30pm.

The excellent *Ta Frenċ* serves rich French cuisine in a converted Gozitan farmhouse. Expect the likes of foie gras with *creme brulée* glaze, veal gel, grilled quail breast and toasted sourdough (€18) or (at the upper end of the scale) the house omelette with lobster, mushroom, leeks and a lobster bisque sauce (€38).

Ta Frenċ

Zafiro

MAP P.104

Xatt ix-Xlendi, Xlendi ☏ 2156 5555. Daily 8am–11.30pm.

A fairly upmarket (but very affordable) restaurant on Xlendi's promenade where homemade pasta and fresh seafood are the stars of the show. The mussels (€10), *fritto misto* (€11) and *garganelli* pasta (€8) are particularly hearty and delicious. The best seats are outside overlooking the turquoise sea.

Bar

Gleneagles

MAP P.104

10 Victory St, Mġarr Harbour ☏ 2155 6543. Daily 2pm–1am.

Opened in 1885, this former fishermen's watering hole is decorated with nautical curios and has a friendly, small town feel. The tables set on the balcony afford good views of the colourful harbour.

Comino

Though it looks like little more than a barren, sun-baked rock from the sea, tiny Comino (just 2km long by 1.7km wide) offers breathtaking clifftop scenery, two of the Maltese islands' most scenic swimming spots, and great snorkelling and diving. The island is a car-free nature reserve and virtually unpopulated, with just one hotel that operates from San Niklaw Bay in the summer, and only three permanent residents. More plentiful than human residents are feathered ones; the island is a haven for migratory birds and birdwatchers, since hunting and trapping are forbidden year round.

From June to September, Comino sees its fair share of visitors and the area around the Blue Lagoon becomes very congested, since a dip in its crystal-clear waters is not to be missed. Shoulder season (October to May) is an ideal time to explore the island by foot, when the rocky habitat blooms into a mosaic of flowers and milder temperatures make hiking comfortable (avoid venturing out in the extreme heat of summer as Comino is nearly treeless and devoid of shade).

The island has been populated at least since Roman times (a full archaeological survey of the island has yet to be undertaken) and was a popular hideaway for corsairs during the time of the Knights, but it was likely most highly populated during Malta's brief French occupation (1798–1800) when the island served as a place of exile and imprisonment for at least 150 criminals and opponents of the regime.

The Blue Lagoon
MAP P.124, POCKET MAP C12

A sweep of bright turquoise water sandwiched between Comino and its sister islet of Cominotto, the

Blue Lagoon

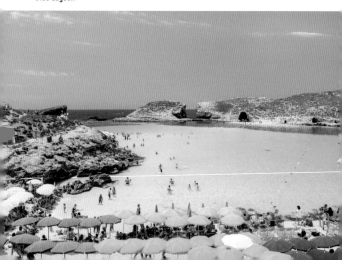

Visiting Comino

The **Comino Ferries Co-Op** (☎ 9940 6529 or 9983 5766, ⓦ cominoferries.com) operates year-round shuttles between Malta's Ċirkewwa ferry terminal or Marfa Resort and Comino's Blue Lagoon or Santa Marija Bay. The shuttles run every 30min in the summer and hourly in the winter. Boats depart for the Blue Lagoon between 9am and 3pm, and return from the Blue Lagoon between 9.30am and 4pm (winter) or 6pm (summer). Boats depart for Santa Marija Bay hourly from 9.30am–4.30pm, and leave for Malta between noon and 4pm (winter) or 6pm (summer).

Ebsons (☎ 7920 4014, ⓦ cominoferryservice.com) also operates a ferry service between Mġarr (Gozo; see page 107), the Blue Lagoon (Comino) and Ċirkewwa (Malta). Boats depart from Mġarr hourly from 8am–6pm, from the Blue Lagoon hourly between 9.30am and 3.30pm (winter) or 6pm (summer) and from Ċirkewwa hourly (winter) or every 30min (summer) between 9.10am and 3.40pm.

The **standard fare** for trips with all companies is €10 return (discounts are usually offered for larger groups). From November to February boats operate sporadically due to low demand, so it's best to call ahead.

Several **tour companies** operate regular trips to Comino from April to October, most stopping in Comino for five hours, which is plenty of time to swim and explore. Captain Morgan is the most popular choice amongst backpackers, with rock bottom prices (☎ 2346 3333, ⓦ captainmorgan.com.mt; €20 including lunch and free bar; April & Nov 10am–4.30pm; May–Oct 10am–5.30pm). Hornblower Cruises are a more comfortable option, with an a/c lounge, basic café facilities and a rooftop lounge area with waterslide (☎ 7909 2764, ⓦ hornblowerboat.com; €20 per person; Mon–Sat 10.30am–5.30pm).

Blue Lagoon is aptly named. The water is crystal clear, and you can enjoy the dramatic vista of the cliffs and Comino's tower as you swim between the islands, but be advised of strong rip currents here yearlong, and lifeguards are only on duty between June and October. The downside is that the Blue Lagoon gets hideously overcrowded in summer, when boats packed with day-tripping tourists anchor in the bay from mid-morning until late afternoon. The small patch of sand fronting the lagoon at both ends is tiny and fills up quickly, and even on sunny winter afternoons some touring boats call at the lagoon. If you're looking for quiet, it's best to visit in the morning on one of the first tour boats of the day. Public toilet facilities are available, and in the summer a number of food trucks offer snacks and ice creams.

St Mary's Tower

MAP P.124, POCKET MAP C12
Open Apr–Oct Wed & Fri–Sun 10.30am–3pm or when the flag is flying.

The sheer cliffs and variegated colours of the deep waters beyond the Blue Lagoon serve as a beautiful backdrop to **St Mary's Tower**. The largest of the Knights' coastal towers, with walls over 5m thick, the tower was built in 1618 by Grand Master Alof de Wignacourt as a base for the garrison of troops stationed on Comino to protect the island from invasion and to guard

Crystal Lagoon

the Malta–Gozo channel. From its roof you can see almost the entire island. Film buffs may recognize St Mary's Tower as Château d'If from the 2002 Hollywood film, *The Count of Monte Cristo*.

Santa Marija Bay

MAP P.124

With inviting turquoise water and a small strip of sand, **Santa Marija Bay** is an ideal alternative to the Blue Lagoon and locals' preferred option for a beach day in Comino. There's good snorkelling among the rocks towards the outer reaches of the bay, and sunbeds and umbrellas can be rented from the kiosk on the beach, which also offers refreshments and shower facilities. There's also a free public campsite between the beach and nearby chapel (follow the signs posted). On the other side of the headland that encloses the bay (and not accessible from land) is a popular **dive site** known as Santa Marija Cave, renowned for its silvery shoals of docile bream, which are happy to eat stale bread from your hands like pets. All Gozo-based dive centres (see page 145) organise trips to the site.

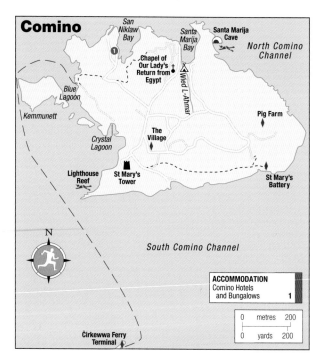

Comino

San Niklaw Bay

Santa Marija Bay

Santa Marija Cave

North Comino Channel

Chapel of Our Lady's Return from Egypt

Wied L-Aħmar

Blue Lagoon

Kemmunett

Pig Farm

Crystal Lagoon

The Village

Lighthouse Reef

St Mary's Tower

St Mary's Battery

N

South Comino Channel

ACCOMMODATION
Comino Hotels and Bungalows 1

| 0 | metres | 200 |
| 0 | yards | 200 |

Ċirkewwa Ferry Terminal

A Comino walking tour

This circular route around Comino, departing from Blue Lagoon in an anti-clockwise direction, takes about two hours. Keep your eyes peeled for wildlife including Maltese wall lizards, wild rabbits and Mediterranean chameleons (not found on Gozo and Malta). You might also come across chunks of rusting iron – reminders that the British used the island for target practice in the early twentieth century.

To begin, head off in the direction of **St Mary's Tower** (see page 123). The path on this part of Comino passes by a string of attractive islets, the **Crystal Lagoon** and Comino's only valley – il-Wied ta' Skalanova. Venture off route into the valley and you'll find a 20m-wide hole in the rocky ground. This is a collapsed limestone cave, called the **Roofless Cave**, the entrance to which can only be seen from the sea. Passing St Mary's Tower you will see **il-Palazz** (the Palace), formerly a colonial-era isolation hospital for plague and cholera victims. By 1948 it housed a community of 65 people who grew export crops on Comino until the early 1960s (you can still see the rubble walls dividing disused farming fields across the island).

Turning right, follow the road constructed by the Knights to connect St Mary's Tower and St Mary's Battery. Erected in 1714, the latter is the best-preserved of the dozens of batteries erected by the Knights in their drive to reinforce Malta's coastal defences. The garigue habitat here supports a hugely diverse array of plants, including musty scented wild thyme and capers, which sport beautiful white-and-purple blooms in spring. Continue straight along Comino's southern coast to arrive at the defensive battery, where the path turns north and leads to **Wied l-Aħmar** (The Red Valley), fringed by native carobs, olives, almonds and Aleppo pines; in the spring, the uncultivated portions of the valley are covered with a carpet of bright yellow Cape Sorrel flowers.

As the valley widens, a pink-coloured outpost built by the Knights in 1743 (now housing Comino's police station) and a diminutive thirteenth-century **chapel** (Our Lady's Return from Egypt) come into view.

Shaded by cypresses and a palm tree, and with timber doors and three bells dangling inside stone hoops, the simplicity of its design – typical of medieval Malta's vernacular architecture – gives the building a striking, evocative appearance. The chapel overlooks **Santa Marija Bay** (see page 124) – continuing along the road beyond the chapel you can turn right at the first crossroads to go to San Niklaw Bay, or press on and return to the Blue Lagoon.

ACCOMMODATION

InterContinental Malta

Accommodation

Hotels and guesthouses book up several months in advance, especially in high season. The average rate for a good four-star hotel in Malta is around €100, and more luxurious options start at €200. The cheapest hotels are in the north, and the most expensive around Sliema, St Julian's and Valletta, which also offer the best transport links. Except in Valletta, most hotels (and some self-catered options) have parking. Unless stated otherwise, all places listed are for the cheapest online double room rate in high season, including breakfast and en-suite facilities; low season rates would be less than half this.

Malta's hostels are quickly catching up to (and often exceeding) its hotels in modern amenities and chic style. The majority are located in Sliema and St Julian's, and are typically a third of the price of even the most affordable hotels (dorms from €18 and double rooms from €50). Most organise group activities and excursions, and many have outdoor pools (where barbecues are hosted during summer nights). Unless stated, prices include breakfast. Self-catering accommodation is a good-value option for groups and families. You'll find budget options in the south and north, and (comparatively) more expensive options in Valletta, Sliema, St Julian's and Gozo. Particularly in Gozo, minimum stay lengths (2–5 days) usually apply. Along with the places listed below, try Airbnb or, for Gozo (where farmhouses are the most popular self-catered option), try ⓦ gozoholidayhomes.com or ⓦ gozovillarentals.com.

Valletta

CASA ELLUL Map p.28, pocket map E6. 81 Old Theatre St, Valletta ☏ 2122 4821, ⓦ casaellul.com. Malta's most exclusive boutique hotel, discreetly located in a Victorian palazzo opposite the Carmelite Church (see page 69), with eight personalised suites designed by young Maltese architect Chris Briffa. Rooms have luxurious touches throughout; expect two-storey ceilings, walk-in showers, espresso machines, Maltese balconies,

Rooms with a view

Author picks

Luxury: *Kempinski Resort* see page 134
Boutique: *Casa Ellul* see page 128
Traditional: *Luciano Al Porto Boutique* see below
Budget: *Inhawi Boutique Hostel* see page 131
Family: *DB San Antonio Hotel & Spa* see page 133

breathtaking bathtubs and one-of-a-kind antiques. Two suites facing the church's impressive dome boast private terraces with Jacuzzis. **€299**

HOTEL CASTILLE Map p.28, pocket map E7. St Paul St, Valletta ☎ 2122 0173, Ⓦ hotelcastillemalta.com. The 38-room Castille is conveniently located between Auberge de Castille and Upper Barrakka Gardens. Rooms are charming, with exposed limestone walls, and most offer lovely piazza views. Facilities include lounges, a restaurant and a beer cave. **€90**

LA FALCONERIA Map p.28, pocket map E7. 62 Melita St, Valletta ☎ 2247 6600, Ⓦ lafalconeria.com. An ultra-modern boutique with all the amenities of a large hotel, just on a smaller scale. The fitness centre, small indoor pool (located in an alluring limestone cistern), rooftop terrace with city views, on-site café, restaurant and 24/7 reception ensure you'll want for nothing during your stay. **€190**

LUCIANO AL PORTO BOUTIQUE Map p.28, pocket map E7. 255 St Ursula St, Valletta ☎ 7725 2977, Ⓦ vallettaboutique. com. Located atop the popular *Bridge Bar* (see page 44), Luciano Al Porto Boutique is easily recognised by its traditional bright red wooden balconies, which means it is perhaps the most photographed guesthouse in Valletta. Rooms are individually decorated with quirky local touches throughout; most offer Grand Harbour views. **€180**

OSBORNE Map p.28, pocket map E7. 50 Triq Nofs In-Nhar, Valletta ☎ 2124 3656, Ⓦ osbornehotel.com. The Osborne offers a spot of British comfort and style in Valletta. A distinctly old-world atmosphere in the lobby gives way to 63 comfortably

furnished rooms and a compact rooftop terrace and pool. **€100**

PALAZZO CONSIGLIA Map p.28, pocket map F7. 102 St Ursula St, Valletta ☎ 2124 4222, Ⓦ palazzoconsiglia.com. A thirteen-room boutique hotel with individually decorated rooms boasting hardwood floors and small lounges. The palazzo's former cellar is now a modern spa with an indoor pool. Two unusual features include a glass elevator in the palazzo's glass-roofed courtyard lobby and a little rooftop plunge pool that overlooks a crimson church dome. **€198**

PALAZZO PRINCE D'ORANGE Map p.28, pocket map E6. 316 St Paul's St, Valletta ☎ 9912 5200, Ⓦ palazzoprincemalta. com. Five luxurious apartments set in a seventeenth-century palazzo, each individually decorated with spacious lounges, kitchens and dining areas. Facilities include a rooftop terrace, a small gym and in-room spa treatments. **€180**

PHOENICIA Map p.28, pocket map D7. The Mall, Floriana ☎ 2122 5241, Ⓦ campbellgrayhotels.com. Valletta's most deluxe hotel was constructed in the 1930s and underwent a major refurbishment in 2017; it is now tastefully decorated in a colonial-meets-Mediterranean style throughout. Facilities are extensive and impossibly elegant, including 7.5 acres of mature gardens and a luxurious infinity pool. This impressive hotel has played host to the likes of Queen Elizabeth II, Alec Guinness and Arnold Schwarzenegger. **€225**

THE SAINT JOHN Map p.28, pocket map F6. 176 Merchant St, Valletta ☎ 2124 3243, Ⓦ thesaintjohnmalta.com. A new 21-room hotel with sleekly styled rooms encircling a sun-drenched interior courtyard. In each, mobile phones can be used to control room temperature and order room service. A stylish on-site gastro pub offers a selection of local beers (and garden swings as seating). €195

SU29 BOUTIQUE HOTEL Map p.28, pocket map E7. 29 St Ursula Steps, Valletta ☎ 2124 2929, ⓦ Su29hotel.com. This stylish boutique hotel might have come straight out of New York or London, offering a striking contrast between original features (wooden beams and exposed limestone walls) and trendy details (marble floors, glass walls). Its eight suites have orthopaedic mattresses, original art and Dermalogica beauty products. €185

TANO'S BOUTIQUE GUESTHOUSE Map p.28, pocket map E7. 41 St Paul St, Valletta ☎ 2703 5907. A pleasant, modern guesthouse set in a traditional townhouse with arched limestone ceilings, exposed wooden beams and original Maltese tiles. All rooms are individually decorated. €180

VALLETTA MERISI SUITES Map p.28, pocket map E7. 48 St Ursula St, Valletta ☎ 7924 0043, ⓦ vallettamerisisuites.com. Sleek, modern, self-catered apartments with kitchenettes and sofa areas, plus a shared terrace and charming furnished courtyard. €115

The Three Cities

BOCO BOUTIQUE HOTEL Map p.48, pocket map G9. 65 Oratory St, Cospicua ☎ 2034 1578, ⓦ bocoboutique.com. A six-room boutique hotel in a four-hundred-year-old Maltese townhouse, located off the beaten path in Cospicua. Rooms are designed by local artists and charming details are abundant, including upcycled furniture. €85

LOCANDA GELSOMINA Map p.48, pocket map G9. 3 Popular Council St, Birgu ☎ 2180 7897, ⓦ locandagelsomina.com. Situated in Birgu's Collachio, this pretty boutique hotel is set in an early sixteenth-century palazzo uniquely accented with Asian art collected during the owner's travels. Four suites are individually and luxuriously decorated. Yoga retreats (2–7 days) and in-house massages are also offered. Minimum stay two nights. €200

Sliema and St Julian's

115 THE STRAND SUITES Map p.56, pocket map C5. The Strand, Sliema ☎ 2131 5030, ⓦ 115thestrand.com. Located 100m away from the Gżira seafront promenade, these apartments are furnished in a comfortable and modern style, with a/c, balconies, kitchens and laundry facilities. €100

BOHO HOSTEL Map p.56, pocket map A4. Villa Cycas, Dun G. Xerri St, St Julian's ☎ 2765 6008, ⓦ bohohostel.com. Boho Hostel lives up to its name, with eclectic style and rainbow-coloured rooms. Its standout feature is the lively garden, with multiple outdoor dining areas, barbecue and hammocks. Shared facilities include a lounge/TV area and kitchen. Dorms €18

CAVALIERI ART HOTEL Map p.56, pocket map B2. Spinola Rd, St Julian's ☎ 2138 0000, ⓦ cavalierihotelmalta.com. There's nothing particularly artistic about this hotel, but it does offer comfortable and affordable rooms, many with expansive views of Spinola and Balluta Bays, plus an outdoor pool that overlooks the sea. €135

CORINTHIA HOTEL ST GEORGE'S BAY Map p.56, pocket map A1. St George's Bay, St Julian's ☎ 2137 4114, ⓦ corinthia.com. The five-star Corinthia is elegantly luxurious with extensive facilities, including six pools, a diving school, water sports and sailing facilities, and a luxury spa. Rooms are classically styled in warm ochre tones. A courtesy bus transports guests to Sliema, St Julian's, Valletta and the Royal Malta Golf Club. Eight on-site restaurants offer a range of tempting options from molecular cuisine to English afternoon tea. €320

THE DISTRICT HOTEL Map p.56, pocket map A1. Triq Santu Wistin, Paċeville ☎ 2741 1441, ⓦ thedistricthotel.com.mt. A chic option on the outskirts of Paċeville. Although the District does not have any facilities, it is considerably more affordable than other hotels in the area. €115

THE GEORGE Map p.56, pocket map A1. Paċeville Ave, St Julian's ☏ 2011 1000, ⓦ thegeorgemalta.com. Situated in the heart of Malta's clubbing district, with a suitably hip design and small rooftop pool. A bright, cheerful lobby leads to basic spa facilities. Rooms are spacious and tranquil. **€160**

HILTON Map p.56, pocket map B2 Portomaso, St Julian's ☏ 2138 3383, ⓦ hilton.com. One of Malta's most sumptuous and glitzy hotels, with an elegant lobby awash in soft greys and twinkling silver chandeliers, plus sumptuously appointed rooms, all with balconies or terraces. The Hilton has three restaurants, four bars, four outdoor pools, a spa, fitness centre, tennis and squash courts, two children's pools and a heated indoor pool. With its crèche club services (fees apply), this a popular hotel for families. **€310**

HOSTEL MALTI Map p.56, pocket map A3. 4 Birkirkara Hill, St Julian's ☏ 2730 2758, ⓦ hostelmalti.com. Located in a converted townhouse, this hostel is a kaleidoscope of colour. Common areas include two shared kitchens, TV lounge and terrace with Jacuzzi. Quiet time begins at 11pm but nightly pub-crawls are organized so you can mix and mingle off-site. **Dorms €20**

HOSTEL MED Map p.56, pocket map A2. Swieqi Rd, 143 The Willows, St Julian's. This designer hostel boasts beautiful local art and common areas, making it popular among mature travellers less keen on Malta's clubbing scene. Common facilities include a roof terrace, barbecue, outdoor shower and TV lounge. **Dorms €25**

HOTEL JULIANI Map p.56, pocket map A2. 25 St George's Rd, St Julian's ☏ 2138 8000, ⓦ hoteljuliani.com. The Juliani's facade retains the look of a typical Baroque townhouse but the interior is refreshingly modern. 47 rooms, thirteen of which are suites, are each appointed with spacious bathrooms and large beds. Facilities include a small gym and luxurious rooftop lounge offering impressive views of Spinola Bay.

Also home to the superb Asian fusion restaurant, *Zest* (see page 62). **€170**

HOTEL VALENTINA Map p.56, pocket map B2. Dobbie St, Paċeville, St Julian's ☏ 2138 2232, ⓦ hotelvalentina.com. A refreshingly modern, 94-room hotel with a sleek lobby, bar and outdoor terraces at ground level. Staff are welcoming and helpful, and rooms are decorated in a minimal but comfortable style. A rooftop lap pool is open from April–Oct. The excellent *Chalice Bar* is located just across the street, and a 2min walk brings you to Malta's main restaurant district and the sea. **€165**

INHAWI BOUTIQUE HOSTEL Map p.56, pocket map B4. Hill St, Balluta Bay, St Julian's ☏ 2138 2554, ⓦ inhawi. com. Overlooking one of the area's only green valleys, Malta's newest and most luxurious hostel has beautiful Scandinavian-inspired interiors that are nicer than many hotels. Facilities include a communal kitchen, small garden with hammock, 24/7 reception and a large pool. **Dorms €32**

INTERCONTINENTAL MALTA Map p.56, pocket map A1. St George's Bay, St Julian's ☏ 2137 7600, ⓦ malta. intercontinental.com. Located in the middle of Malta's clubbing district, the 480 rooms at the InterContinental are tastefully and luxuriously decorated. Facilities include a kids' club, fitness centre, squash courts, hair salon, business centre, lagoon-style outdoor swimming pool, heated indoor swimming pool, spa and glitzy rooftop infinity pool. "Luxury Highline Suites" include butler service, and all guests enjoy access to the nearby InterContinental Beach Club. **€180**

ONYX SUITES & APARTMENTS Map p.56, pocket map B2. 2 Ross St, Paċeville ☏ 2137 8700, ⓦ onyxmalta. com. Onyx Suites, located in the heart of the clubbing district of Paċeville, offer well-appointed apartments with warm furnishings, free wi-fi, kitchen with dishwasher, large balconies, TV and a/c. **€105**

THE PALACE Map p.56, pocket map D4. High St, Sliema ☎ 2133 3444, ⓦ thepalacemalta.com. The Palace is part-boutique, part-large hotel, with six distinctly themed suites, nine junior suites and an additional 145 modern rooms. Suites offer quirky details (think 1950s jukeboxes). There's also an on-site spa, fitness centre, indoor/outdoor pools and several good restaurants. Unlike most hotels in Sliema, it's situated in the village centre: a 5min walk brings you to the sea and Malta's main shopping district. **€185**

PEBBLES BOUTIQUE APARTHOTEL Map p.56, pocket map C4. 88 The Strand, Sliema ☎ 2131 1889, ⓦ pebbleshotelmalta.com. A modern seafront apart-hotel above a popular string of bars and restaurants. Apartments have a/c, kitchens and lounges. Superior apartments also have spacious sea-view terraces. Hotel-style amenities include 24hr reception, a rooftop terrace with Jacuzzi, and free access to the nearby MedAsia lido (see page 58). **€110**

PV HOSTEL Map p.56, pocket map A1. 13 Wilga St, St Julian's ☎ 7942 9687, ⓦ maltahostels.com.mt. Modern, shared accommodation in the heart of Paċeville. Expect to hear noise from nearby clubs 24/7, but rooms are comfortable, cheap and modern with free wi-fi, a/c and no curfew. Dorms **€32**

THE VICTORIA Map p.56, pocket map C4. Ġorġ Borg Olivier St, Sliema ☎ 2133 4711, ⓦ victoriahotel.com. As its name might suggest, the Victoria blends sleek Mediterranean and British style. Facilities include a compact gym and outdoor pool. A charming pub, *The Penny Black*, serves local lager by the pint alongside proper fish and chips. **€160**

WESTIN Map p.56, pocket map B1. Dragonara Rd, St Julian's ☎ 2138 1000, ⓦ westinmalta.com. Situated on the coast at the outskirts of Paċeville, this attractive pink building oozes old-school style and charm. Central but secluded, the Westin is an ideal base for exploring Malta while intermittently soaking up the sun at its indoor/outdoor pools or two private beaches. If you're visiting on the weekend, the lobby bar is an ideal spot for afternoon tea. A glitzy casino is located on site. **€200**

Mdina and Rabat

POINT DE VUE Map p.66. 2 Saqqajja Square, Rabat ☎ 2145 4117, ⓦ pointdevue-mdina.com. A modest but comfortable fifteen-room guesthouse located on a public square-cum-car park just outside of Mdina's fortified walls. Several rooms at this seventeenth-century converted palazzo offer sweeping countryside views. On the ground floor, a busy family restaurant serves up rustic fare. **€105**

XARA PALACE RELAIS & CHATEAUX Map p.66. Misraħ Il-Kunsill Mdina ☎ 2145 0560, ⓦ xarapalace.com.mt. Set in a seventeenth-century palace, this intimate and impossibly romantic hotel is one of Malta's best (and a favourite of Hollywood celebrities). An elegant lobby is arranged around a central courtyard, with creeping ivy and a glass roof. Most rooms are duplexes with one-of-a-kind antiques, king-sized beds, and a full range of modern facilities. Those at the back have sweeping views of northern Malta, and some boast terraces with Jacuzzis. An outdoor pool is located at the nearby Xara Lodge, a 5min drive away (courtesy shuttles provided). Two top-notch restaurants include the exquisite De Mondion (see page 73). **€235**

Central Malta

CORINTHIA PALACE HOTEL & SPA Map p.76. De Paule Ave, San Anton, Balzan ☎ 2144 0301, ⓦ corinthia.com. Set across from the San Anton Gardens (see page 74) in the manicured suburbs of central Malta, this Grande Dame offers a pleasant respite from the chaos of Malta's main tourist areas. Rooms are classically decorated with a touch of intimacy and homeliness. Mature gardens provide a picturesque setting for two pools, four restaurants and a "Zen" spa. **€140**

The north

DB SAN ANTONIO HOTEL & SPA Map p.84, pocket map G11. Tourist St, Qawra ☎ 2158 3434, ⓦ dbhotelsresorts.com. This all-inclusive resort is one of the largest in Malta, with five hundred rooms and suites. Its exterior is imposing and bland, but the huge range of facilities includes two outdoor pools, an adults-only rooftop pool and deck, a private sandy beach, a kids'/teens' area with animators, free dance and aqua sport classes, five restaurants, two bars, a spa and gym. For such a large resort, the rooms are surprisingly pleasant, with a modern Moorish theme. San Antonio's sister hotel, the DB Seabank Resort & Spa, is located in nearby Mellieħa and offers similar facilities, but rooms (same price) follow a nautical theme. Four nights minimum stay. **€185**

DOLMEN RESORT HOTEL Map p.84, pocket map G11. Dolmen St, Buġibba ☎ 2158 1510, ⓦ dolmen.com.mt. Beneath the dated exterior of this large resort is a surprisingly modern lobby and a range of facilities including four pools, a private beach, indoor pool, luxury spa, gym, casino, diving club and public lido Amazonia (see page 86). Rooms are awash in dull browns and beiges, but comfortably appointed; some have large terraces. **€165**

MARITIM ANTONINE Map p.88. Ġorġ Borg Olivier St, Mellieħa ☎ 2152 0923, ⓦ maritim.com.mt. An attractive cream-and-maroon building in Mellieħa's town centre, designed to look like a series of townhouses. Rooms lack a personal touch, but are modern and spacious (some also have balconies). Facilities include a swimming pool in small but lush gardens, and an on-site spa. A rooftop restaurant offers stunning views of Mellieħa's parish church and Għadira beach. **€130**

PARK LANE APARTHOTEL Map p.84, pocket map G11 Maskli St, Qawra ☎ 2157 7319, ⓦ parklanemalta.com. The adults-only Park Lane Aparthotel offers six self-catering apartment types. Rooms are bright and airy, with free wi-fi, sleek kitchenettes and a small dining area and lounge. There's also an outdoor pool. **€110**

RADISSON GOLDEN SANDS Map p.80. Golden Bay, Mellieħa ☎ 2356 1000, ⓦ radissonblu.com. The five-star Radisson Golden Sands is the most luxurious in the north. The resort comprises 144 rooms and 164 suites furnished in a slightly bland but modern style. Four restaurants, a luxury spa, a private beach, pools, child-minding services and water sports mean you'll never have to leave the resort – and panoramic views of Golden Bay mean you may not want to. **€330**

SALINI RESORT Map p.84, pocket map H11. Salina Bay, St Paul's Bay ☎ 2157 3781, ⓦ saliniresort.com. This large resort recently benefitted from a top-to-bottom refurbishment, and now boasts 237 bright and airy rooms, with a/c, TV and private balconies. Four restaurants, including a superb pizzeria, are located on site. Self-catering rooms with kitchenettes are also an option. Resort facilities include a luxury spa, fitness centre, indoor heated pool, tennis courts, and two outdoor pools, one of which is a palm-tree-lined infinity pool with expansive views of St Paul's Bay. **€130**

SPLENDID GUEST HOUSE Map p.88. 42 Il Kappillan Magri St, Mellieħa ☎ 2152 2536, ⓦ splendidmalta.com. A funky, family-run guesthouse with fourteen brightly coloured rooms (most have a/c and all have private showers). The bohemian theme continues throughout the guesthouse's common areas, including a chill-out area on the roof. **€63**

The south

DUNCAN GUESTHOUSE Map p.100. 32 Xatt Is-Sajjieda, Marsaxlokk ☎ 2165 7212, ⓦ duncanmalta.com. Set adjacent to Marsaxlokk's parish church, this guesthouse has ten studio apartments. Although quite rustic, they are spacious with fridge, coffee machine, toaster, sink, a/c and TV. Some also have balconies overlooking Marsaxlokk's colourful harbour. **€60**

PORT VIEW GUESTHOUSE Map p.100. Luzzu St, Marsaxlokk ☎ 9907 6004, ⓦ portview. A comfortable guesthouse with thirteen modern and spacious rooms, including quads for families. Breakfast is served on the guesthouse's rooftop terrace with harbour views. €90

QUAYSIDE APARTMENTS Map p.100.
1 Fisherman's Wharf, Marsaxlokk ☏ 9949 1852, ⓦ quarsidemalta.com. Charming street-level apartments located in a converted nineteenth-century townhouse, with colourful front doors that match those of nearby fishing boats. Charming rustic features include exposed limestone walls, wooden ceiling beams and patterned Maltese floor tiles. Each apartment is equipped with TV, kitchenette, laundry facilities, living room and interconnecting bedrooms. Apartments share a common garden. €50

Gozo

B&B DAR TA' ZEPPI Map p.104. 39
28th April 1688 St, Qala ☏ 2155 5051, ⓦ dartazeppi.com. A friendly Belgian artist and her Gozitan husband run this quaint five-room B&B. Rooms feature local art, colourful tiled floors and tall, wooden-beamed ceilings. Common facilities include a swimming pool, garden, and table tennis. Yoga, meditation and art workshops are also offered. €150

DOWNTOWN Map p.106. Europe St,
Victoria ☏ 2210 8000, ⓦ downtown. com.mt. The rooms here are in need of refurbishment, but come with large beds. Facilities include a tiny rooftop pool, a children's play zone and a garish bowling alley. A strategic and affordable place to stay if you lack private transport: in summer, free transport is offered to beaches, and Victoria is Gozo's transport hub. €75

THE DUKE BOUTIQUE HOTEL Map p.106.
Republic St, Victoria ☏ 2779 9100, ⓦ thedukegozo.com. A modern boutique hotel located on the fourth and fifth floors of the Duke Shopping Complex, next to Victoria's pretty Villa Rundle Gardens (see page 105). Rooms, awash with marble, command views of the Citadel or have a private terrace with Jacuzzi. Its location is unbeatable, with frequent transport links. €110

ELLIE BOO BED & BREAKFAST Map
p.108. 104 Ballura St, Xaghra ☏ 2156 0626, ⓦ bbgozo.com. Run by a British family, shared facilities at this homely B&B include an outdoor pool, lounge with TV and a hammock-slung garden with views of Gozo's verdant valleys. €100

GOZO ESCAPE Map p.108. Various
locations, Gozo ☏ 7941 9405, ⓦ gozoescape.com. These fourteen beautiful farmhouses located throughout Gozo each sleep a minimum of four. Most are over three-hundred years old and all have outdoor pools, a/c and wood-burning fireplaces. Seven nights minimum stay in July/August. €115

GRAND HOTEL Map p.104. Sant
Antnin St, Mġarr ☏ 2156 3840, ⓦ grandhotelmalta.com. An imposing hybrid of Baroque and Neoclassical design overlooking Mġarr harbour. Rooms are comfortably furnished in a classic style and have a/c and TVs. A large range of facilities includes cinemas, a games room, a basic gym and an outdoor swimming pool with impressive views. €80

KEMPINSKI SAN LAWRENZ RESORT Map
p.114. Rokon St, San Lawrenz ☏ 2211 0000, ⓦ kempinski.com. Gozo's most luxurious resort, and undoubtedly one of the country's best. The lobby boasts coffered wooden ceilings and superb contemporary art, while the best of the rooms have sizeable terraces from which you can see Dwejra's bright green terraced fields just beyond the hotel's grounds. Mature gardens are a major draw – fragrant flowers, palm trees and water features surround three spotlessly clean pools, and vegetable allotments provide fresh ingredients for three top-notch restaurants and an impressive breakfast buffet. The hotel's luxury spa offers two indoor pools, steam chamber and Ayurvedic treatments. Courtesy shuttles offer easy access to top sites. €270

MARIA GIOVANNA GUEST HOUSE Map
p.108. Rabat Road, Marsalforn. Lying a 2min walk from Marsalforn beach, this fifteen-room guesthouse offers double rooms (some with sea views) in a typically

rustic Gozitan style with pine furniture, wrought-iron beds and quirky bric-a-brac. €60

MURELLA LIVING B&B Map p.108. 18 Oven St, Marsalforn ☎ 2155 0340, ⓦ murellaliving.com. The best value for money in Marsalforn, this colourful, ultra-modern B&B feels very much like a boutique hotel, with large designer rooms. €80

QUAINT HOTELS Map p.104. 13 December St, Nadur ☎ 2210 850, ⓦ quainthotelsgozo.com. Twelve spacious, ultra modern rooms (including three penthouses) in the heart of Nadur village life. A second location in Xewkija (ten rooms) is equally as pleasant. €75

TA ĊENĊ Map p.104. Ċenċ St, Ta Sannat ☎ 2155 6819, ⓦ tacenchotel.com. Once a grand five-star hotel attracting Hollywood celebrities, the Old-World-style Ta Ċenċ has become rundown recent years, but still offers a pleasantly secluded atmosphere

and an extensive array of facilities, including indoor/outdoor swimming pools, tennis courts, and a private beach at the magnificent Mgarr ix-Xini (see page 109). Guest rooms, which are more pleasant than common areas, are housed in stone bungalows with private terraces or gardens. Courtesy shuttles service main sites. Three nights minimum stay in high season. €270

Comino

COMINO HOTELS AND BUNGALOWS Map p.124. San Niklaw Bay, Comino ☎ 2152 9821, ⓦ cominohotels.com. The only accommodation on Comino is ideal if you're looking for complete isolation. The hotel offers 95 rooms (49 of which have sea views), each with a/c. Facilities include tennis courts, a gym, diving and snorkelling activities and various restaurants and bars. 46 detached bungalows (some with multiple beds) are part of the same complex, situated in adjacent Santa Marija Bay. Open May–Oct only. **Half board €62**

ESSENTIALS

Carnival

Arrival

International flights arrive at Malta International Airport, around 8km (20min drive) south of Valletta. There's a **taxi stand** at the arrivals terminal; a list of standard fares is posted and fares are paid in advance at the designated ticket counter. Approximate fares are €17 to Valletta, €20 to Sliema and St Julian's, and €28 to Buġibba or Ċirkewwa. Public **buses** stop just outside the departures terminal and service all regions frequently (daily 5.30am–10pm; €1.50 winter, €2.00 summer). There's also a direct bus (X1; 1hr journey) to the Gozo **ferry** at Ċirkewwa. For detailed bus schedules visit the Malta Public Transport kiosk in the arrivals hall (daily 8am–7.30pm).

Getting around

By bus

With an extensive and cheap network of **buses**, it's relatively easy to explore Malta and Gozo via public transport. Malta's fleet of public buses are modern and air-conditioned and call at three main hubs: Valletta, Sliema, the airport in Luqa, and the ferry terminal at Ċirkewwa. Services start at 5.30am and run until 11pm; on Fridays and Saturdays a night bus service departs from Paceville, the main clubbing district, between midnight and 3am. During the summer months, an extra night bus service departs Ta Qali, where Malta's major outdoor clubs are located, between 11pm and 4am. Night bus services cost €3 per trip. Buses are numbered and full **route maps and schedules** can be found on ⓦ publictransport.com.mt, on the free Tal-Linja app, and on Google Maps. Hard copies of bus schedules and maps of bus routes are also available from tourist offices and bus stations.

Bus tickets (€1.50 Nov–May, €2 June–Oct, €3 night routes, yearlong) can be purchased in cash from your bus driver, or at a sales and information office, which are located at the Valletta bus terminal, Sliema ferries terminal, Malta International Airport, Mater Dei hospital, Buġibba bus terminal and Victoria bus terminal. **Bus passes** called "Explore Cards" for unlimited travel are sold at the bus stations; they're valid for seven days and cost €21 for adults, or €39 including two trips on the Valletta-Sliema-Birgu ferry services and a hop-on hop-off bus tour or boat trip to Comino. You can also purchase a block of twelve one-day travel tickets for €15; these can be used yearlong.

Most buses are equipped with an automated audio system to announce upcoming stops. If you're in doubt, drivers are normally happy to tell you where to get off.

By car

The downsides of **renting a car**, aside from the expense, are the poor road conditions in rural areas and the chaotic local driving habits. To rent a car or a motorbike, you'll need to present a valid driving licence, and you must be over 21. You may also need to show your passport, and some firms ask for a cash deposit or credit card imprint. An optional extra €5–7 for comprehensive insurance cover is worthwhile considering Malta's high accident rates; otherwise, damage to the vehicle can incur the insurance excess of €350. Average rates for a four-door car – about €30–60 per day – are usually discounted if you rent for longer than five days (local companies typically offer cheaper rates than international brands). All of the following companies can arrange for cars to be picked up and left at the airport or other locations, and in all cases you can get a quote, book and pay via their website: Aquarius Rent A Car (117 St Paul's Street, St Paul's Bay ☎ 2157 5736, ⓦ aquariusrentacar.com); Budget (50 Msida Seafront, Msida ☎ 2123 3668, ⓦ budget.com.mt); Thrifty (Malta

International Airport Arrivals lounge ☎2131 4636, ⊛thrifty.com); Goldcar (Malta International Airport ☎2744 7512, ⊛goldcar.es); Hertz (Malta International Airport ☎2131 4636, ⊛hertz.com. mt); Mayjo Car Rentals (Triq Fortunato Mizzi, Rabat, Gozo ☎2155 6678, ⊛mayjocarhire.com); Rabat Garage (92 Triq Kola Xagħra, Rabat ☎2145 3975, ⊛rabatgarage.com.mt); Sixt (Malta International Airport Arrivals lounge ☎2182 1416, ⊛sixt.com).

By scooter, quad bike or bicycle

To rent a **scooter**, the minimum age requirement is 18–23 (depending on company and bike size). A 125cc moped in high season costs €35 per day. Drivers must hold a driving licence (most rental scooters in Malta are 125cc), and most companies require a refundable €200–300 security deposit. If you rent a scooter, bear in mind that bends can be slippery (because of dust/oil build-up). Watch out for potholes and wear a helmet (usually provided by the rental company). **Quad bikes** are particularly popular in Gozo. Gozo Quad Hire (Borg Għarib St, Għajnsielem, Gozo ☎2156 4031, ⊛gozoquadhire. com) offers them at €80/9hr or €60/day for two days or more (drivers must be 21 or older). In Malta, Tony's Rentals (46 The Strand, Sliema ☎2134 1695, ⊛carrentalmalta.eu) offers quads from €90/day. Alternatively, try AHS Malta (200 San Albert St, Gżira ☎2134 0149, ⊛ahsmalta.com).

Ecobikes Malta (8 Imsel St, Buġibba ☎2750 0022, ⊛bikerentalmalta.com) offers **mountain bike** rentals (from €15/day; €40/3 days) and ebike rentals (from €20/day; €55/3 days) against a €50–100 deposit. For beginners, Gozo Adventures (7 Saint Indrija St, Victoria, Gozo ☎9999 4592, ⊛gozoadventures. com) also offers guided **bicycle tours** (€65/day, including guide and lunch). Most reputable providers offer helmets, locks, and repair kits at no extra charge. Although rural areas of Gozo and Malta can be pleasant to explore by bike, and distances are short, the topography is hilly and the summer heat can be exhausting. If you're interested in renting a bicycle for transport within and between villages, **Next Bike** (€1.50 for the first 30min; €1 for each additional 30min, €16/day) is a good option. Malta's national bicycle rental service has self-service terminals across the island at major tourist centres (Valletta, Sliema, St Julian's). Register at any terminal or on the Next Bike app, which provides a code to unlock your bicycle. Bicycles can be returned at any terminal in the network. Bear in mind motorists are still growing accustomed to sharing the road with cyclists – exercise extreme caution and stick to the seafront to avoid exhausting hills. Helmets are not provided with Next Bikes. Other bike rental outlets include Mike's Rent a Bike (95 The Strand, Sliema ☎2733 4335, ⊛mikesrentabikemalta.com) and The Cyclist (Rihan St, San Ġwann. ☎2766 1166, ⊛thecyclistmalta.com).

By taxi

Official **taxis** are white and have their registration number painted on the side of the car. There are plenty of strategically located **taxi stands** in the central areas, with main stands at the airport, Valletta bus terminal, Bisazza Street Sliema, Buġibba. Though taxis have meters, they're rarely used, and fares are often arbitrary – in most cases, drivers will try to squeeze as much money out of you as possible (for a stomach-rolling ride, to boot). Expect to pay €15 from Valletta to Sliema and €25 from Sliema to Buġibba. The airport is the only place where white taxi fares are fixed and strictly enforced (€17 to Valletta, €20 to Sliema/St Julian's, €35 to Buġibba/Ċirkewwa). After the buses have stopped running at about 11pm, taxi prices generally go up by about a third. Several companies offer a slightly more expensive but considerably more comfortable 24hr service with free wi-fi and SMS notifications – good options include eCabs (☎ 2138 3838, ⓦ ecabs. com.mt), Yellow Cabs (☎ 2298 2298, ⓦ yellowcabsmalta.com) and Greenr (electric cars, ☎ 2738 3838, ⓦ greenr. cab). Haggling isn't necessary with these operators; you'll be quoted a fixed fare online or by phone (€20 from the airport to Valletta, €15 from Valletta to Sliema, €19 from Sliema to Buġibba and €34 from the airport to Ċirkewwa). In Gozo you'll find white taxis at Mġarr Harbour and in Victoria at the bus station and Independence Square, but at night you won't find taxis anywhere and you would have to pre-arrange with a chauffeur-driven service – try Mayjo in Rabat (☎ 2155 6678 or ☎ 2155 1772).

Directory A–Z

Addresses
House and building numbers are uncommon in Malta. Houses and buildings are typically referred to by names (e.g. 'Santa Marija' house) or simply by their street name or nearby landmarks. To confuse matters further, English and Maltese street names are used interchangeably (for example, Triq and Street). To inform a taxi driver of your destination, a street name and village name (or, even better, just a hotel name) is usually sufficient. The correct mailing address format in Malta is: [Number] [Street Name] [Village] [Postcode]. Postcodes can be found online at ⓦ postcodes.maltapost.com.

Cinema
All mainstream cinemas have modern theatres and generally feature Hollywood releases. Tickets cost between €5 and €7. Options include the two-screen Ċittadella Theatre (17 Castle Hill, Victoria, Gozo ☎ 2155 9955, ⓦ citadelcinema.com); the thirteen-screen Eden Century Cinemas (St. George's Bay, St Julian's ☎ 2371 0400, ⓦ edencinemas.com.mt); the six-screen Embassy (Saint Lucy Street, Valletta ☎ 2122 2225, ⓦ embassycomplex. com.mt); and the seven-screen Empire Cinema Complex (Pioneer Road, Buġibba ☎ 2158 1787, ⓦ empirecinema.com.mt).

Crime
Malta has a very low crime rate, and remains one of those rare places where many locals don't even lock their front doors. Even in busy tourist areas, pickpocketing and theft are not very common. Exercise common sense while exploring (lock your car doors, mind your luggage, protect your passport) but you needn't wear a money belt or wear your backpack on your front. Walking alone at night is safe in nearly all areas, and CCTV is in use in public spaces.

Electricity
The supply is 240V; plugs are three-pin.

Embassies and consulates
UK High Commission (Whitehall Mansions, Ta Xbiex Seafront ☎ 2323 0000); US Embassy (Ta Qali National Park, Attard ☎ 2561 4000); Canada Consulate (Demajo House, 103 Archbishop St, Valletta ☎ 2552 3233);

Emergencies
For police, ambulance and fire service, call ☎ 112; for air rescue call ☎ 2124 4371 (☎ 2182 4220 outside office hours, including weekends); for sea rescue call ☎ 2123 8797. If you're involved in a traffic accident call Local Wardens on ☎ 2132 0202.

Australia High Commission (Ta' Xbiex Terrace, Ta' Xbiex ☎ 2133 8201).

Health

Hospitals: Mater Dei (University Heights, Msida ☎ 2545 000); Gozo General Hospital (Victoria, Gozo ☎ 2156 6000).

Internet

Free wi-fi is available in public squares and gardens (look for the MCA free network).

Laundry

There are a handful of strategically located laundries, some with coin-operated machines. Malta's largest company, Portughes, has four main outlets and five pick up/drop off points within stationery shops and convenience stores, including one in Sannat, Gozo; they do pick-ups and deliveries from any address (☎ 2144 4444, ⊕ portughes.com).

Left luggage

Most hotels in Malta offer free luggage storage. You can also store luggage at the Malta International Airport's Departures Hall (open 24/7, up to €12 for hand luggage and €14 for large luggage for each 24-hour period. Presentation of valid ID is required and valuable items, such as personal electronics, are not accepted).

LGBT+

Over the last few years, Malta has experienced a definite and positive shift towards greater acceptance of LGBT+ in all aspects of life. It is a very safe destination for LGBT+ travellers and number one on the European Rainbow Index. Gay Guide Malta (⊕ gayguidemalta.com) offers a wealth of information on events, gay-friendly accommodation and the best entertainment venues. LGBT+ friendly bars and clubs include *AXM*

(St George's Rd, Paċeville; Wed–Sun 10pm–4am); *Michelangelo Club Lounge* (St Rita's Steps, Paċeville; daily 10pm–4am); *The Birdcage Lounge* (Triq il-Kbira, Rabat; Mon–Fri 10pm–3am, Sat & Sun 10pm–4am); *Rubies* (Triq Sant Andrija, San Ġwann; Tues–Sun 7pm–1am); and *Monaliza Lounge* (Great Siege Rd, Valletta; Mon–Thurs noon–2am, Fri–Sun noon–4am).

Lost property

You can reclaim lost property at the **Malta International Airport** (where it's held for 30 days) Mon to Fri 7.30am to 4pm at its main Customer Service desk. Lost property (especially wallets) is frequently turned in to police, so it's worth filing a report. To report other lost property or a suspected theft, visit a Police Station or call ☎ 2122 4001. You can also file police reports online for lost property valued at less than €250 at ⊕ pulizija.gov.mt/opres.

Money

Malta's **currency** is the euro. Most **banks** open Mon to Sat from 8.30am–2pm; in towns, you'll never be more than a ten-minute walk from one, and all branches have ATMs (in Gozo, however, there are only ATMs in Victoria, Nadur, Mġarr and Marsalforn). Banks offer the best rates for cash or travellers' cheques; exchange bureaux normally charge a higher commission of about three percent, though their opening hours tend to be more convenient, while hotels charge a similar commission and round off the exchange rate to their advantage. All major credit cards – Visa, Mastercard, American Express, Diners, as well as others – are widely accepted by shops, hotels, guesthouses and car rental companies, but it's best to carry some cash as smaller restaurants and cafés may not accept cards.

The cost of living and visiting Malta is rising. Supermarket prices reach

EU averages, and a two-course meal excluding drinks in a restaurant will cost around €25; alcoholic drinks, however, are cheaper than in most European countries. Public transport is €2 per trip, and entry fees for sights and museums are €5–€0 (a Heritage Malta multi-site pass offers access to all 22 museums and sites for €50). Accommodation will be your biggest expense (see page 128).

Opening hours

High street shops in Malta are generally open **Mon–Sat 9am–7pm**. Small or family-run shops usually close between 1pm and 4pm Mon–Fri, and at 1pm on Saturday. Almost all shops and supermarkets in Malta are closed on Sundays, with the exception of Arkadia supermarket (Portomaso Complex, St. Julian's; Sun 8am–10pm), Scotts supermarket (Triq Amery, Sliema; Sun 8.30am–12.30pm) and Bay Street shopping complex (open daily 10am–10pm). Restaurants are open from 7pm for dinner Mon–Sat, and from noon to 3pm for lunch daily. Museums and galleries are generally open daily 10am–5pm, with last admissions from 4.30pm.

Pharmacies

The islands' many **pharmacies** open Mon–Sat 9am–7pm. Daily newspapers and ⓦ pharmacy.com.mt list those that open, on a roster basis, during evenings, Sundays and public holidays until 10pm. Pharmacies sell over-the-counter medicines, contact lenses and emergency contraception.

Phones

The **international dialling code** for Malta is +356. There are plenty of telephone booths scattered throughout Malta, but most take phone cards that you buy from souvenir shops. SIM cards can be purchased at any GO (15 Bisazza St, Sliema ☎ 7922 2146; Mon–Sat 9.30am–7pm) or Vodafone outlet (Malta International Airport ☎ 9999 9247; daily 9am–9pm) from €20 including 1GB of data and €5 in calling credits.

Post

There's a **post office** in virtually every town on the islands, most open Mon–Sat 8am–noon, but the two main offices – in Valletta and Rabat, Gozo – stay open until 4pm. International mail is dispatched on the next working day; to the UK it takes three days; seven to ten days to North America; and up to two weeks for Australia and New Zealand.

Smoking

Smoking in public places is banned, but this is very loosely enforced. There's even smoking inside some night clubs. Cigarettes can be purchased from vending machines, located in most bars and some cafés.

Theatre

There are four theatres in the Maltese islands and the season runs between Oct and May. Check at tourist offices for details of upcoming events, or keep an eye out for posters, as well as listings on theatre websites. Offerings are fairly varied, from mainstream touring productions to plays by Maltese companies, while theatres are also used to stage classical music concerts, opera and ballet. The Astra Theatre (9 Republic St, Victoria, Gozo ☎ 2155 6256, ⓦ teatruastra.org.mt) is Malta's largest Baroque theatre and features anything from operas to drama and ballet. The large Aurora Opera Theatre (100 Republic St, Victoria, Gozo ☎ 2156 2974, ⓦ teatruaurora.com) is renowned for excellent operas; it also stages drama and other events such as ballet. The eighteenth-century Manoel Theatre (115 Old Theatre St, Valletta ☎ 2122 2618, ⓦ teatrumanoel.com.mt) is Malta's national theatre, and features drama and concerts. Theatre in the

Round (St James Cavalier, Pope Pius 5 St, Valletta ☎ 2122 3200, ⌨ kreattivita. org) is a small theatre with sixty seats arranged around the central stage.

Time

Malta is **one hour ahead of GMT** and observes daylight saving time.

Tipping

Locals round up to the nearest euro on a small bill or leave a 5–10% gratuity for a larger group. Tourists are expected to tip more (around 10%, you can leave it on the table). Tipping is not strictly required for taxi drivers or tour operators, and is usually only used to reward excellent service. Tipping (a few euro) is expected for valets and bus boys.

Tourist information

Local and overseas offices of the Malta Tourism Authority supply leaflets on sights and activities, as well as free maps and an annual calendar of events; staff can help with basic queries, and all local offices have lists of accommodation options. In some offices (such as at the airport), they can help you book accommodation on the spot. There are offices in the following places: Airport Arrivals Hall (☎ 2369 6073; daily 10am–9pm); 28 Melita Street, Valletta (☎ 2122 0193; Mon–Sat 9am–5.30pm, Sun 9am–1pm); 17 Independence Square, Rabat, Gozo (☎ 2291 5452; Mon–Sat 9am–5.30pm, Sun 9am–1pm); Birgu Inquisitor's Palace (Main Gate Street ☎ 2180 0145; Mon–Sat 9am–5pm, Sun 9am–1pm); Marsaxlokk (Xatt is-Sajjieda ☎ 2165 1151; Mon–Sat 9am–5.30/6pm & Sun 9am–2pm); Mdina (St Publius Square ☎ 2145 4480; Mon–Sat 9am–5.30pm, Sun 9am–1pm); Mellieħa (Misraħ iz-Zjara tal-Papa Ġwanni Pawlu II ☎ 2152 4666; Mon–Sat 9am–1pm); Buġibba (Islets Promenade ☎ 2141 9176; Mon–Sat 9am–5.30pm, Sun 9am–1pm); Sliema (Info Desk Plaza

Shopping Centre ☎ 2136 3691; Mon–Sat 9.30am–6pm).

The Malta Tourism Authority's **website** for Gozo, ⌨ visitgozo.com, provides an overview of all major sites, attractions and activities, and a calendar of events. Malta Tourism Authority's website, ⌨ visitmalta.com, provides useful practical information and a calendar of events.

Travellers with disabilities

Planning rules have only had to make provision for people with disabilities in the last decade, and facilities generally remain rather poor. Many upmarket hotels have specially equipped rooms and most public buses can accommodate wheelchairs. The Yellow Cab company offers wheelchair-friendly taxis (☎ 2298 2298, ⌨ yellowcabsmalta. com; €18 from Valletta to Sliema). The National Commission for Persons with Disabilities (Bugeia Institute, Braille Street, Santa Venera ☎ 2278 8555, ⌨ knpd.org; Mon 8.15am–noon & 1.30–5pm, Tues–Fri 8.15am–noon) is focused on fostering a national framework for people with disabilities, not providing general information, though you can contact them if you're stuck or need any information and assistance.

Travelling with children

Malta is a child-friendly destination, but it can be tricky to manoeuvre prams on the narrow streets of most villages. Sliema and St Julian's are the best bases for families, with their extensive promenades and newer and larger playgrounds at ix-Xatt ta' Qui-Si-Sana (near the main shopping district), Independence Gardens (also called Exiles, on Triq it Torri) and in Pembroke (Triq G. Portanier). Most public museums are free for children, while private attractions offer discounts.

Sports and outdoor activities

Watersports

Watersports outfits operate on many of the island's' main beaches between May and Oct, and offer everything from parasailing (€40/flight), water skiing or wakeboarding (€50/20min), paddle boarding (€20/hr), jet-skiing (€40/15min), banana rides (€8/10min) or jet pack hoverboarding (€60/25min) to canoes and kayaks (€6/hr). Many also have self-driving speedboats for rent (€25–80/hr; no licence required). Reputable watersport companies include Sun & Fun (Corinthia Beach Resort, St George's Bay; ☎ 2137 3822, Ⓦ sunfunmalta.com) and Oh Yeah Sports (Tunny Net Complex, Mellieħa; ☎ 9930 0040, Ⓦ ohyeahmalta.com).

Snorkelling

With some of the clearest water in the Mediterranean, shallow and glassy-calm in the summer, Malta boasts some superb snorkelling. A large concentration of marine life can be found in the nooks and crannies along the entirety of the islands' rocky shores. Underwater rocks harbour clusters of spiny sea urchins, inquisitive common octopus and beautiful red starfish. Finger-sized fishes such as blennies, grey triggerfish and Connemara suckerfish float in shallow waters, darting away as you get close to explore their variegated colours. Large, silvery shoals of fish are also commonly seen close to the shoreline – these include bream, mullet, silverfish, sand smelt, chromis and wrasse. Recommended and conveniently situated snorkelling hotspots include the Exiles area in Sliema, and Golden Bay and Għajn Tuffieħa beaches. Further afield, Għar Lapsi and Mġarr ix-Xini (Gozo) are sure bets — but just about anywhere you take a dip in Malta you're likely to find the fish plentiful and the snorkelling satisfying.

Scuba diving

Malta's waters offer some of the best scuba diving in the Mediterranean, and attract some 50,000 enthusiasts annually. Aside from stunning seascapes (from boulder meadows, to wartime wrecks, gulleys, labyrinthine caves, chimneys and ledges to sheer cliff-drops), underwater visibility is excellent here – 20m in spring and autumn during plankton build-up, and up to 45m between Nov and March – while the mild weather allows year-round diving (water temperatures rise to a peak average of 27°C in summer, and go down to just 15°C in winter). Shore and boat dive sites are scattered across the archipelago, but of the three islands, Gozo offers the most spectacular dive sites, especially off Dwejra at the western tip (the Blue Hole in Dwejra rates in Jacques Cousteau's top 10 worldwide). The basic rule of thumb is that the further north you go, the better the diving. Lawson and Leslie Wood's *The Dive Sites of Malta, Comino and Gozo* contains detailed information (available online).

The diving centres scattered throughout the islands are professional outfits affiliated with the major international schools (PADI, CMAS, BSAC, SSI Advanced Open Water, etc) and offer all the standard courses plus specialized programmes such as night- or cave-diving, as well equipment rentals. Five-day open water courses start from around €250, and advanced open water courses start from €400. Most schools also offer taster dives for the uninitiated – instructors take you down to a depth of up to 10m without the need of prior instruction (around

€45–60). You can join the diving centres in escorted or group dives (around €20 per dive, including equipment), or, if you're a qualified diver, you can rent equipment and dive independently. In this case, bear in mind that some dives can be tricky for those not used to local conditions; fatal incidents are reported yearly in caves off Dwejra in Gozo, when silt stirs up and obscures the caves' mouths.

Diving centres

MALTA

Dive Malta Dive Centre St Julian's Aquatic Sports Club, George Borg Olivier St, St Julian's ☎ 2136 9994, ⊛ divemalta.com.mt. Daily 8am–6pm.

Dive Systems Tower Point, Tower Rd, Sliema ☎ 2131 9123, ⊛ divesystemsmalta.com. June–Sept: daily 8.30am–6.30pm; Oct–May: Mon–Sat 8.30am–5pm.

Dive Wise Westin Dragonara Complex, St Julian's ☎ 2135 6441, ⊛ divewise.com.mt.

Go Dive Malta 2 Triq Dun Grangisk Sciberras, Mellieħa ☎ 2755 0182, ⊛ godivemalta.co.uk.

Maltaqua Mosta Rd, St Paul's Bay ☎ 2157 1111, ⊛ maltaqua.com. May–Nov: daily 7.30am–5.30pm; Dec–April: daily 8am–4pm.

GOZO

Calypso Diving Centre Triq Marina, Marsalforn Bay Seafront ☎ 2156 1757, ⊛ calypsodivers.com.

Gozo Aqua Sports Rabat Rd, Marsalforn ☎ 2156 3037, ⊛ gozoaquasports.com.

Moby Dives Xlendi Bay ☎ 2155 1616, ⊛ mobydivesgozo.com. Daily 9am–6pm.

Scuba Kings Dive Centre 46 Santa Maria St, Marsalforn ☎ 9923 0788, ⊛ divemalta-gozo.com.

Hiking

The network of paths that criss cross the Maltese countryside offer ample opportunity for hiking. We've detailed some short, scenic walks in the guide, but for longer hikes, head to Malta's south coast between Dingli Cliffs and Ras Il-Qammiegħ, or to Gozo's coastal cliffs between Mġarr Ix-Xini and Xlendi, Xlendi and Ras Il-Wardija, and San Blas Bay and Marsalforn. Visit Malta offers excellent, detailed and free walking guides with maps for these and other routes in English, French and German (⊛ visitmalta.com).

The best time for hiking in Malta is winter (Oct–May), when the weather is mild and the landscape green. In summer, you'll find that only early morning or evening walking is comfortable (or, indeed, safe) and the parched countryside isn't that appealing. Bear in mind that during autumn and spring (and particularly in April and May), bird-hunters can be a nuisance; besides shattering the peace with shotgun blasts, hunters can get tetchy with strollers, largely because they are aware that non-hunters may disapprove. Although incidents are rare, if you encounter a hunter the most prudent thing to do is to greet him affably and keep going. It's also good to note that it's not always clear what land in the countryside is public or private, and even public access roads are frequently cordoned off with makeshift (illegal) signs or gates. The Tourism Information Office provides excellent guidance on accessible routes, as do local hiking groups. You can join the Ramblers Association (☎ 9949 7080, ⊛ ramblersmalta.org) on one of its free walks for hikers of all levels – up to seven monthly – between October and May (detailed programmes of walks are on the website). Another possibility is to walk with MC Adventures (☎ 7751 4963, ⊛ mcadventure.com.mt) who organise private, tailor-made walks.

Festivals and events

Carnival

Staged during the week preceding Lent, Valletta and Floriana's carnival parades feature large neon-coloured floats and professional dance troupes that compete for awards. Nadur in Gozo sees pre-Lenten celebrations that are closer to the mock-revolutionary origins of carnival, in which the underclasses romped through the streets in an unruly display. Although modern influences are evident (you'll see lots of latex Halloween-style masks), the unorganised street theatre and performances are still driven by the original spirit, and many of the costumes are farcical parodies of the powers-that-be. Be aware that the scenes (and costumes) in Nadur can get bawdy and rowdy. Carnival weekend is one of the busiest times of the year in Gozo; unless you book months in advance you're unlikely to find accommodation, and ferry queues can be lengthy.

Easter

Each Good Friday, many Maltese towns stage sober biblical re-enactments. Starting at dusk, these impressive parades feature Biblical characters and statues representing the Stations of the Cross. Participants dress in white robes and hoods, and drag bundles of metal chains or wooden crosses, in penitence and holy self-mortification. The best re-enactments are held in Xagħra (see page 112), Żejtun (see page 98) and Valletta (see page 26). On Easter Sunday, towns all over Malta erupt in celebration, and events include sprinting with the statue of the Risen Christ to symbolise Christ's Resurrection – the most raucous events are held in Birgu (see page 46) and Xagħra after morning Mass at around 10am. Easter marks the beginning of high season tourism on the islands.

International Fireworks Festival

April ⓦ maltafireworksfestival.com
Usually hosted during the last week of April in Gozo and Malta, the International Fireworks Festival sees fireworks producers compete against each other with elaborate pyro-musical displays. Shows are always free and locations change every year, but typically the festival ends in a grand finale over the Grand Harbour in Valletta (best viewed from St Barbara's Bastions or Barriera Wharf).

Malta Music Week

June ⓦ isleofmtv.com
The last week of June is dedicated to clubbing in Malta with the Isle of MTV Malta Music Week bringing in top international acts for performances at Malta's largest open-air clubs. The week culminates in a huge free concert in Floriana.

Għanafest

June ⓦ festivalsmalta.com
This two-day folk music festival takes place every year in June in different public gardens throughout Malta. The festival takes its name from Għana, a form of traditional Maltese folk singing.

Malta Jazz Festival

July ⓦ maltajazzfestival.com
Malta's annual three-day jazz festival hosted in mid-July at beautiful Barrier Wharf, Valletta. For over ten years, the Grand Harbour has offered an atmospheric backdrop for local and foreign acts including Diana Krall, Natalie Cole, Chick Corea, Wayne Shorter and Mike Stern. Most events are ticketed (€25–50) but if you're only interested in a casual look, performances can be clearly heard and seen from atop St Barbara's Bastions.

Public holidays

Malta has fourteen public holidays: Jan 1, Feb 10, March 19, Good Friday, March 31, May 1, June 7, June 29, Aug 15, Sept 8, Sept 21, Dec 8, Dec 13 and Dec 25.

Wine Festivals

July and August Ⓦ delicata.com, Ⓦ marsovinwinefestival.com

Each summer, Valletta hosts two wine festivals from local producers Marsovin (July) and Delicata (August). The Marsovin Festival is held at Hasting's Gardens over three nights, and offers the biggest venue with the best wines. Entrance is free and you pay for drink tokens. The Delicata Wine Festival is hosted later in the summer at Upper Barrakka Garden, a smaller (more crowded) venue with superb views. This event is all-you-can-drink for the price of a commemorative wine glass.

Notte Bianca

October Ⓦ festivalsmalta.com

Like other White Nights across Europe, Valletta's Notte Bianca is a nocturnal contemporary arts festival. Typically hosted on the first Saturday of October or the last Saturday of September, it sees over a hundred free artistic and musical performances unfold across Valletta. The event kicks off around 8pm and wraps up by 3am. The official programme of events is usually announced a month in advance.

Birgufest

October

This celebration of Birgu's beauty, history and culture is one of Malta's top annual events, hosted during the first weekend of October. The festival sees the village lit by hundreds of thousands of candles, often at their most abundant in the front parlours of Birgu's townhouses, where they are tucked into heaps of religious bric-a-brac. Front doors are thrown wide open for the public to enjoy the spectacle; a reminder of the warm hospitality (and low crime rates) on the island.

Malta Classic

October Ⓦ maltaclassic.com

The Malta Classic is a four-day celebration of vintage style and classic cars hosted every October in Mdina. Local car collectors (of which there are a surprising number for such a small island) compete to win races in various categories. For tourists, the main draw of the event is the Concours d'Elegance, usually hosted on the Friday, which sees collectors in period dress showcasing their automotive gems in the village's picturesque square.

Christmas

December

From December 8th (a public holiday) onwards, locals start heading to Valletta to take in the beautiful light displays, do their Christmas shopping and enjoy a glass of mulled wine. Many parishes, as well as individuals, put up impressive mechanised cribs (called *presepju* in Maltese). In the weeks leading up to the big event, the entire Gozitan village of Għajnsielem is transformed into an immersive re-enactment of Bethlehem, complete with dozens of volunteer actors playing the essential roles in the Christmas story. The religious build-up climaxes on Christmas Eve when most Maltese attend a ritualized version of High Mass at midnight, after which many families have a 2am "Christmas breakfast". On Christmas Day, families celebrate with elaborate multi-course meals including soup, lasagna, pasta, turkey and heaps of desserts and wine.

Chronology

c. 5000 BCE Neolithic people arrive in Malta from Sicily.

3600 BCE The first of the Neolithic temples – the oldest extant buildings in the world – is constructed at Ġgantija, Gozo.

3300 BCE The Hypogeum of Ħal-Saflieni is constructed in present-day Tarxien, followed by the Tarxien Temple complex.

2500 BCE The Neolithic period comes to an inexplicable end.

2000 BCE Bronze-Age settlers inhabit Malta, erecting fortified castles and granaries on ridges and hills.

800–480 BCE The Phoenicians turn the island into a centre for sea trade. Mdina is established as Malta's first town and is to remain the capital for a millennium.

480 BCE–218 CE Malta falls under the control of Carthage.

60 Christian tradition holds that St Paul is shipwrecked in Malta on the way to his trial in Rome, and the first seeds of Christianity on the island are sown.

218 After several wars between Carthage and Rome, the latter finally consolidates its rule in Malta.

395–870 After the split in the Roman Empire, Malta falls under Byzantine rule.

870 Aghlabid Arabs coming from North Africa capture Malta, and Islamic rule begins – a period whose lasting legacy is the development of the Maltese language, architecture and irrigation systems that are still practised today, besides the introduction of orange and lemon trees.

1090–1530 Malta swings under the influence of a dizzying number of various rulers, including the Normans, Aragonese, Swabians and Angevins, as well as various regional strongmen and merchants who run the islands as their private fiefdom.

1530 Charles V of Spain gives Malta to the Knights of St John (now the Knights of Malta) in return for a Maltese falcon every year. The Knights, in retreat after being routed out of Rhodes by the Ottomans in 1522, put Malta on the frontline of the Muslim–Christian struggle for supremacy and territory. They establish their base in Birgu.

1551 Dragut Rias, an Ottoman general, attacks Malta with his fleet. The Knights repel the attack, and Dragut raids Gozo instead; he breaches the Ċittadella and almost the entire population is taken as slaves.

1565 Dragut leads a second attack with a massive show of force, but after his death and a war of attrition lasting six months, the Ottoman army is defeated in what's now known as the Great Siege of 1565.

1566 Work begins on Valletta, Malta's new fortified capital city.

1570 The Knights relocate their base to Valletta and begin construction on the city's most glorious auberges, palazzos and St John's Co-Cathedral. Their rule on the islands persists for two more centuries.

1798 Aided by treacherous Knights, Napoleon Bonaparte takes Malta in three days of light skirmishes;

the Knights are forced to leave and Napoleon loots most of their riches to pay for his wars. Napoleon is in Malta for six days, during which time he abolishes feudal rights and slavery, establishes a Government Commission, public finance administration and the foundations for today's public judicial and education systems. Three months after the arrival of the French, the deeply Catholic Maltese revolt as the French have been closing convents and seizing church treasures. French forces retreat to Valletta, and the Maltese insurgents – aided by the British Army – lay siege; it takes two years before the starving French soldiers surrender.

1800 The British take possession of the islands.

1835 Britain rules the islands as a colony, and sets up a Maltese Council of Government that advises the British governor.

World War I Britain turns Malta into the "Nurse of the Mediterranean", a centre for recuperating injured soldiers.

1919 Protests for greater autonomy from the British turn violent (British troops fire into a crowd, killing four). Britain moves fast to defuse the tension, resulting in a Maltese government with limited autonomy being established in 1921.

World War II Malta is the Mediterranean headquarters for the British Navy. With its submarines disrupting the Axis supply routes to Africa, the island is subjected to a long and intense aerial bombardment – one of the worst in history. By 1942, Malta is pushed to the brink of starvation and surrender. In a last-ditch effort, Operation Pedestal brings in supplies that carry Malta through its darkest hour. Malta's contribution to World War II is recognized with the George Cross – the only time the medal has been awarded to an entire nation.

1964 Malta gains independence from Britain as a constitutional monarchy.

1974 Malta becomes a Republic. All titles of nobility are abolished.

1979 The last British and NATO troops are ejected from Malta by Dom Mintoff's socialist government, and Malta formally becomes a Non-Aligned Country.

2004 Malta joins the European Union as a full member.

2008 Malta adopts the euro and becomes part of the Schengen visa (open-borders) area within the EU.

2017 Malta loses one of its most famous landmarks, the Azure Window, which crumbles into the sea.

Language

Malti ("Maltese" in English) has its roots in the Arabic of western North Africa, but has gathered many words and influences from Italian, English, French, German and Spanish; in fact, it's a mishmash of all these languages. Though a Semitic language, Maltese is written in a Roman script that evolved at the beginning of the twentieth century: Italian was Malta's default language up to 1934, when it was officially replaced by Maltese and English. Virtually everyone speaks excellent English, and many street signs, shop names, restaurant menus and so on are in English only. Most Maltese speak a hybridized form of Maltese-English in everyday discourse, and a sizeable minority speak English only. Given this situation, the locals don't expect you to attempt to speak Maltese. It's fine (and certainly not offensive) to stick to English, and just learn the basics of Maltese pronunciation in order to get to grips with place names.

The Maltese alphabet has 29 letters – five vowels (as in English) and 24 consonants (some of which will be new): a, b, ċ, d, e, f, g, ġ, h, ħ, i, j, k, l, m, n, għ, o, p, q, r, s, t, u, v, w, x, ż, z. Pronunciation of most of the letters differs from English, in that emphasis is placed on a drawn-out twang, resulting in a sing-song rhythm of conversation. Instances of markedly unusual pronunciation are listed below.

Maltese pronunciation

ċ as **ch** in church
e as in bet
g is hard, as in **g**oat
ġ is soft, as in **j**oke
h is silent (except at the end of a word, when it's pronounced like ħ)
ħ is strong and definite, as in **h**ail
i as the English e in b**ee**
j as in **y**es

għ is silent in most instances
q is a glottal stop – the sound in the beginning and middle of "uh-oh" or the sound of the two ts in the cockney pronunciation of "bottle"
x is an English "sh", as in **sh**ear
ż is soft, as in **z**ebra
z as in ba**ts**

Glossary

aljotta traditional fish soup
awguri best wishes / happy birthday
auberge an inn of residence for a group of Knights forming a particular Langue
baħar sea
bajja bay
bieb generic name for a door or doorway; also the gate to a fortified city
bigilla a dip made of local broad beans
bonġu good morning
bonswa good evening
bragioli a traditional baked dish of steak with a mincemeat stuffing
cavalier tower within fortifications that acts a raised gun platform and rearguard position
ċaw so long, like the Italian ciao
corsair sea-based pirate licensed by the state to carry out piracy against a defined enemy
dagħjsa boat
demi-bastion a small bastion with one flank
fat ladies generic term for well-endowed stone figures and statues from the Neolithic era
festa generally refers to the three-day summer festivals held to commemorate parish saints; also public holidays
fejn where?
forn bakery
fortizza fort
garigue rugged stretches of rocky landscape with pockets of soil that support plant life
ġbejna small round cheese made from local sheep's or goat's milk
għar cave
għassa tal-pulizija police station
għolja hill
globigerina local limestone used in many Maltese buildings
ġnien garden
Grand Master the absolute ruler of the Knights of Malta

grazzi thank you (**grazzi hafna** means thank you very much)

gvern government

gżira island

ħobża bread roll or loaf of bread

ħut fish

il-belt city, usually applied to Valletta

spiżerija pharmacy

iva yes

jekk jogħġbok please

karrozza car

kastell castle

kemm how much?

knisja church

lampuka (singular **lampuki**) dolphin fish or mahi mahi, traditionally fished in early to late autumn

Langue a grouping of the Knights of Malta, defined by the region from which they originated

le no

luzzu colourful vernacular wooden fishing boats

misraħ square or clearing

mużew museum

parroċċa parish

pastizzi (singular **pastizz**) puff pastry pocket stuffed with mushy peas or ricotta

periklu danger

pjazza town square or piazza

posta post office

pulizija police

saħħa literally translates to health or good health, also used to mean good bye

San or **Sant'** (female **Santa**) saint

skużani excuse me / sorry

spnotta sea bass

sqaq alley

tabib doctor

tal-linja bus

tempju shrine, usually in reference to a Neolithic temple

torri tower

triq street or road

vapur ship

wied valley

SMALL PRINT

Publishing Information
First edition 2018

Distribution
UK, Ireland and Europe
Apa Publications (UK) Ltd; sales@roughguides.com
United States and Canada
Ingram Publisher Services; ips@ingramcontent.com
Australia and New Zealand
Woodslane; info@woodslane.com.au
Southeast Asia
Apa Publications (SN) Pte; sales@roughguides.com
Worldwide
Apa Publications (UK) Ltd; sales@roughguides.com
Special Sales, Content Licensing and CoPublishing
Rough Guides can be purchased in bulk quantities at discounted prices. We can
create special editions, personalised jackets and corporate imprints tailored to
your needs. sales@roughguides.com.
roughguides.com
Printed in China by RR Donnelley Asia Printing Solutions Limited

A catalogue record for this book is available from the British Library
The publishers and authors have done their best to ensure the accuracy and
currency of all the information in **Pocket Rough Guide Malta**, however, they can
accept no responsibility for any loss, injury, or inconvenience sustained by any
traveller as a result of information or advice contained in the guide.

Rough Guide Credits
Editor: Tom Fleming
Cartography: Katie Bennett
Picture editor: Aude Vauconsant
Cover photo research: Nicole
Newman

Managing editor: Rachel Lawrence
Senior DTP coordinator: Dan May
Head of DTP and Pre-Press:
Rebeka Davies
Original design: Richard Czapnik

Author: Jess Gerrow. After running one of Malta's first travel blogs and (briefly)
appearing on reality TV, Jess put her pen to this book and her grit into running an
advertising agency. Jess lives in Malta with her husband, two sausage dogs and
436,947 other people.

Acknowledgements
For my husband, without whom Malta would be (to me) unknown.
For the privilege of choosing this island as home.

Help us update

We've gone to a lot of effort to ensure that the first edition of the **Pocket Rough Guide Malta** is accurate and up-to-date. However, things change – places get "discovered", opening hours are notoriously fickle, restaurants and rooms raise prices or lower standards. If you feel we've got it wrong or left something out, we'd like to know, and if you can remember the address, the price, the hours, the phone number, so much the better.

Please send your comments with the subject line "**Pocket Rough Guide Malta Update**" to mail@uk.roughguides.com. We'll credit all contributions and send a copy of the next edition (or any other Rough Guide if you prefer) for the very best emails.

Photo Credits

(Key: T-top; C-centre; B-bottom; L-left; R-right)

Aaron Briffa/viewingmalta.com 21B, 22C, 23T

Alamy 14B, 15T, 17T, 18B, 20B, 53, 68, 70, 76, 108, 117, 118, 120, 125

Alessandro Saffo/4Corners Images 1, 24/25

Anthea Hamilton & Nicholas Byrne/ Malta Contemporary Art 39

Brian Grech/InterContinental Malta 126/127

Brian Grech/The Barracuda 2BR

Caffe Cordina 18C

Chen Weizhong/viewingmalta.com 23C

Christian Kober/John Warburton-Lee Photography Ltd/AWL Images 2BL

Christian Kober/Robert Harding 12B

Clive Vella/viewingmalta.com 99

Denise Wilkins/viewingmalta.com 119

DOMENIC AQUILINA/EPA-EFE/REX/ Shutterstock 35

Dragana Rankovic/Bongo Nyah 103

Dragana Rankovic/Hole in the Wall 63

Dragana Rankovic/La Mère 42

Essence 93

Getty Images 4, 11B, 14T, 16, 18T, 18TC 21C, 69, 72, 77, 95

Infinitely Xara 73

iStock 19B, 32, 40, 47, 58, 59, 64, 65, 87, 97, 101, 107, 111, 116, 122, 124

Janos Grapow & Daniele Cavadini/ Luna The Restaurant 79

Jonathan Xuereb/Christine X Art Gallery 60

Jürgen Scicluna/viewingmalta.com 11T, 17B, 19T, 50, 85

Jürgen Scicluna/MTA 115

Katja Kreder/imageBROKER/Robert Harding 2CR

Malcolm Debono/viewingmalta.com 10

Mario Galea/MTA 21T, 66

Mario Galea/viewingmalta.com 136/137

Mark Cassar 45

Mike Watson Photography/ viewingmalta.com 54

Mithna 91

Nick Ledger/AWL Images 26

Norbert Vella/One80 92

Peter Oliver Vanicsek/viewingmalta. com 2T

Piccolo Padre 62

Picfair 5

Reuben Piscopo/Cek Cik 41

Sabine Lubenow/LOOK/Robert Harding 15B

Shutterstock 22C, 55, 71, 75, 78, 86, 102, 112, 113

Sylvaine Poitau/Apa Publications 88, 121

Terronne 6

Victor Pasmore Gallery 31

viewingmalta.com 6, 12/13T, 13C , 13B, 16B, 19C, 20T, 22C, 22B, 23B, 36, 81, 94, 110

The Malta Classic Car Museum/ viewingmalta.com 82/83

Cover Boat in Marsaxlokk harbour **Massimo Borchi/Atlantide Phototravel**

Index

ROUGH
GUIDES

ESCAPE
THE EVERYDAY

ADVENTURE BECKONS
YOU JUST NEED TO KNOW WHERE TO LOOK

Long bus journey?
Phone run out of juice?

👉 TEST **YOUR KNOWLEDGE** WITH OUR ROUGH GUIDES TRAVEL QUIZ

1 Denim, the pencil, the stethoscope and the hot-air balloon were all invented in which country?

a. Italy
b. France
c. Germany
d. Switzerland

2 What is the busiest airport in the world?

a. London Heathrow
b. Tokyo International
c. Chicago O'Hare
d. Hartsfield-Jackson Atlanta International

3 Which of these countries does not have the equator running through it?

a. Brazil
c. Indonesia
b. Tanzania
d. Colombia

4 What is the principal religion of Japan?

a. Confucianism
b. Buddhism
c. Jainism
d. Shinto

5 Every July in Sonkajärvi, central Finland, contestants gather for the World Championships of which sport?

a. Zorbing
b. Wife-carrying
c. Chess-boxing
d. Extreme ironing

6 What colour are post boxes in Germany?

a. Red
b. Green
c. Blue
d. Yellow

7 For three days each April during Songkran festival in Thailand, people take to the streets to throw what at each other?

a. Water
b. Oranges
c. Tomatoes
d. Underwear

 For more quizzes, competitions and inspirational features go to **roughguides.com**